A PAR
The Northern Wastes
Far Snows
The Snow Wastes
Sea of Snows
reat Valley Reaches
Oakenhulls
Alone
rik's
aven
Strand
Goblin's Teeth Mts
Quench-heart Keep
Druath Glennan
Dwellings of the Fey
Crow river
Dwarrowhame
Sea of The Star
Harith-si-the-Crow
Zarik Golid
Bury of
ur Friths
Fortune Pass
Goth
Storm Giant's Causeway
Jonalbion
Glastondale Abbey
Mts of Vision
Mt Gwalodrun
Fiendil
Trollfens
Sundial
Fortune river
Beyond the Rift
he Manmarch
Irsmuncast nigh Edge
The Rift (Bowels of Orb)
Greenfens
Mortavalon
veneg
Barrow Swales
Spires of Foreshadowing
Doomover
Greyguilds-on-the-Moor
River Greenblood
Hills
Horngroth
Horn Mts
Mt Star-reach
Desolation of the Serpent
Marshes
Walls of Shadow
Great Plateau
Mayhem
Wilderness
Tor
VALLEY OF THE LICH-KINGS
Greydawn
City of the Runes of Doom
Forest
River Greybones

THE WAY OF THE TIGER

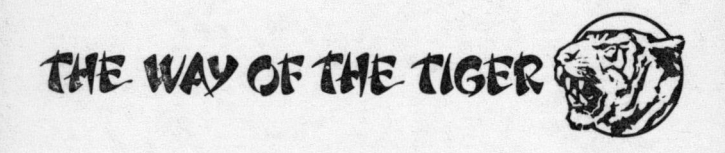

About the authors

Mark Smith was born in Birmingham and brought up in Brighton. He went on to take a degree in experimental psychology at Oxford. Since then he has spent some time in America.

Jamie Thomson was born in Iran and met his co-author whilst at school in Brighton. After taking a degree in politics and government at Kent University he had a variety of jobs before becoming assistant editor of the leading adventure game magazine.

The authors' interest in adventure games began some ten years ago and Mark began work on creating the fantasy world of Orb in 1976.

ASSASSIN!, the second Way of the Tiger title is available now.

WARNING

Do not attempt any of the techniques or methods described in this book. They would result in serious injury or death to an untrained user.

* * *

Historical note

Ninjas are historical fact. Ninjas existed in Japan from the sixth century AD to the beginning of the seventeenth century. For much of this period there were struggles for power between the warlords or diamyos who were the heads of the noble clans. The Ninjas were unknown faceless men, professional assassins and spies, killing machines available for hire. All of the abilities and skills attributed to the Ninja in this book are based on reality. Historically, the Ninjas of Medieval Japan were apparently able to perform most of the feats and were expert in many of the skills outlined in The Way of the Tiger.

THE WAY OF THE TIGER
AVENGER!

Mark Smith and Jamie Thomson

Illustrated by Bob Harvey

KNIGHT BOOKS
Hodder and Stoughton

Copyright © Mark Smith and Jamie Thomson 1985
Illustrations copyright © Hodder and Stoughton Ltd 1985

First published by Knight Books 1985
Eighth impression 1989

British Library C.I.P.

Smith, Mark
 The way of the tiger.
 Avenger!
 1. Games – Juvenile literature
 2. Adventure and adventurers –
  Juvenile literature
 I. Title II. Thomson, Jamie
 793'.9   GV1203

ISBN 0-340-37787-9

The characters and situations in this book are entirely imaginary and bear no relation to any real person or actual happening.

This book is sold subject to the condition that it shall not, by way of trade or otherwise, be lent, re-sold, hired out or otherwise circulated without the publisher's prior consent in any form of binding or cover other than that in which it is published and without a similar condition including this condition being imposed on the subsequent purchaser.

No part of this publication may be reproduced or transmitted in any form or by any means, electronically or mechanically, including photocopying, recording or any information storage or retrieval system, without either the prior permission in writing from the publisher or a licence, permitting restricted copying, issued by the Copyright Licensing Agency, 33–34 Alfred Place, London WC1E 7DP.

Photoset by Rowland Phototypesetting Ltd. Printed and bound in Great Britain for Hodder and Stoughton Paperbacks, a division of Hodder and Stoughton Ltd., Mill Road, Dunton Green, Sevenoaks, Kent TN13 2YA (Editorial Office: 47 Bedford Square, London WC1B 3DP) by Richard Clay Ltd., Bungay, Suffolk.

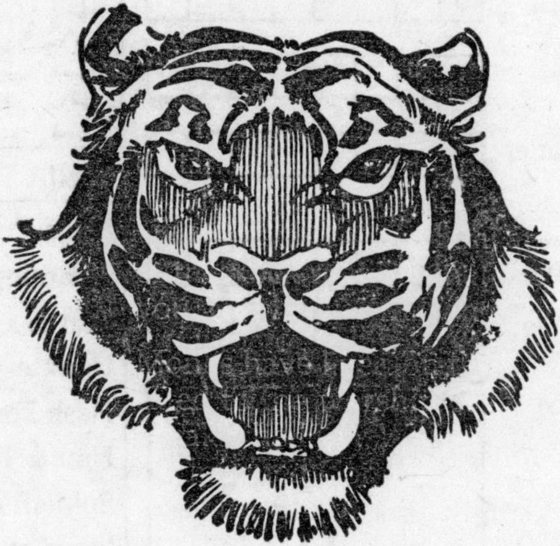

NINJA CHARACTER SHEET

COMBAT RATINGS

Punch | 0 |

Kick | 0 |

Throw | 0 |

Fate Modifier | 0 |

Inner Force | 5 |

Endurance | 20 |

SHURIKEN

☆ ☆
☆
☆
☆

NINJA TOOLS

Ninja Costume
Breathing Tube
Iron Sleeves
Garotte
Flash Powder
Flint & Tinder
Spiderfish
Blood of Nil

NOTES

SPECIAL ITEMS

OPPONENT ENCOUNTER BOXES

Name:
Endurance:

Name:
Endurance:

Name:
Endurance:

Name:
Endurance:

Name:
Endurance:

Name:
Endurance:

Name:
Endurance:

Name:
Endurance:

Winged Horse Kick

Leaping Tiger Kick

Forked Lightning Kick
1
2

Iron Fist Punch

Tiger's Paw Punch

Cobra Strike Punch

Whirlpool Throw

1

2

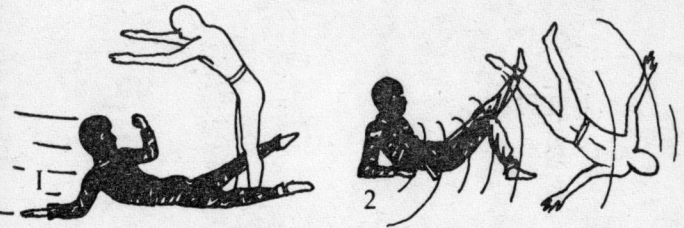

Dragon's Tail Throw

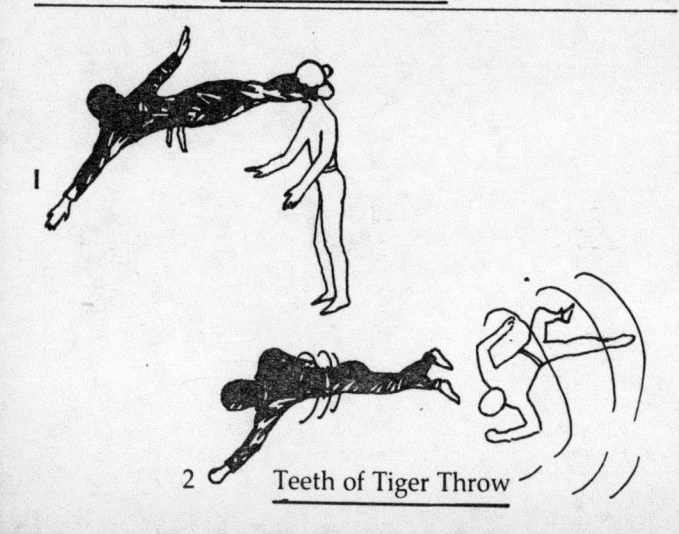

2

Teeth of Tiger Throw

1

2

BACKGROUND

On the magical world of Orb, alone in a sea that the people of the Manmarch call Endless, lies the mystical Island of Tranquil Dreams.

Many years have passed since the time when, as an infant, you first saw its golden shores and emerald rice meadows. A servant brought you, braving the distant leagues of the ponderous ocean from lands to which you have never returned. Your loyal servant laid you, an orphan, at the steps of the Temple of the Rock praying that the monks would care for you, for she was frail and dying of a hideous curse.

Monks have lived on the island for centuries, dedicated to the worship of their God, Kwon, He who speaks the Holy Words of Power, Supreme Master of Unarmed Combat. They live only to help others resist the evil that infests the world. Seeing that you were alone and needed care, the monks took you in and you became an acolyte at the Temple of the Rock. Nothing was made of the strange birthmark, shaped like a crown which you carry on your thigh, though you remember that the old servant insisted that it was of mystical importance. Whenever you have asked about this the monks have bade you meditate and be patient.

The most ancient and powerful of them all, Naijishi, Grandmaster of the Dawn, became your foster-father. He gave you guidance and training in the calm goodness of Kwon, knowledge of men and their ways and how to meditate so that your mind floats free of your body and rides the winds in search of truth.

From the age of six, however, most of your time has

been spent learning the Way of the Tiger. Now, you are a Ninja, a master of the martial arts and a deadly assassin who can kill the most powerful enemies unseen and unsuspected. Like a tiger, you are strong, stealthy, agile, patient in the stalking of prey and deadly. In the Land of Plenty and the Manmarch the fabled Ninja, known as the 'Men with no Shadow', are held in awe – the mere mention of Ninja strikes fear into people's hearts. But you are one of the few who worship Kwon and follow the Way of the Tiger. You use your skill as a bringer of death to rid the world of evil-doers.

At an early age you hung by the hands for hours on end from the branches of trees to strengthen your arms. You ran for miles, your light-footed speed enough to keep a thirty foot ribbon trailing above the ground. You trod tightropes, as agile as a monkey. Now you swim like a fish and leap like a tiger, you move like the whisper of the breeze and glide through the blackest night, like a shade. Before he died Naijishi taught you the Ninja's Covenant.

NINJA NO CHIGIRI

'I will vanish into the night; change my body to wood or stone; sink into the earth and walk through walls and locked doors. I will be killed many times, yet will not die; change my face and become invisible, able to walk among men without being seen.'

It was after your foster-father, Naijishi's death that you began to live the words of the Covenant. A man came to the island, Yaemon, Grandmaster of Flame. Using borrowed sorcery he tricked the monks into believing that he was a worshipper of Kwon from the Greater Continent. He was indeed a monk but he worshipped Kwon's twisted brother, Vile, who helps the powerful to subdue the weak, and wicked men to rule fools. Yaemon slew Naijishi – no one could match him in unarmed combat and he stole the Scrolls of Kettsuin from the Temple. Once more you knew the pain of loss for you had loved Naijishi as a father. You swore an oath to Kwon that one day you would avenge his death. You have honed your skills helping the downtrodden in the Land of Plenty but now the time has come to prove yourself to your brother monks at the Temple of the Rock.

COMBAT

As a Master of Taijutsu, the Ninja's art of unarmed combat, you have four main ways of fighting. Throwing Shuriken (see under skills), kicks, punches or throws. You will be told when you can use Shuriken.

In general it will be harder to hit an opponent when kicking but a kick will do more damage. A throw if successful, will allow you to follow up with a possible 'killing blow', but if you fail a throw your Defence against an opponent will be lower, as you are open to attack. Whenever you are in a combat you will be asked which type of attack you wish to make. See the Way of the Tiger Illustrations for the different types of kicks, punches and throws available to you. You will be told which paragraph to turn to, depending on your choice. When you are resolving combat, you will find it useful to record your opponent's Defence and Endurance score. A number of Encounter Boxes are provided with your Character Sheet for this purpose.

The combats have been presented in such a way that it is possible for you to briefly examine the rules and begin play almost immediately. However, if you do this, don't forget about Blocking and Inner Force, as you won't be told when to use these in the text.

PUNCH

You will be told what Defence number your opponent has against a punch. Roll two dice, and if the score is higher than his or her Defence number, you have successfully punched your opponent. In this case, roll one more die. The result is the amount of damage you have inflicted on your opponent. Subtract it from his Endurance totals. If this has reduced your opponent's score to 0 or less, you have won. When your opponent attacks you, you will be given your Defence number for that combat. Roll two dice, if the score is greater than this number, you have been hit. The amount of damage inflicted upon you depends on the opponent and will be noted in the paragraph. Usually in the format of 'Damage: 1 Die + 1' or '2 Dice' or '1 Die + 2'. Simply roll the required number of dice and add the number given. This is the total damage inflicted upon you. However before you subtract this score from your Endurance, you may choose to try and block or parry the attack (see Block).

Punch Modifier

Whenever you make a 'Punch Roll' to determine whether or not you have successfully struck an opponent, add or subtract your Punch Modifier. This Modifier reflects your skill in using the punches of the Way of the Tiger. You begin with a

Punch Modifier of 0, as noted on your Character Sheet. This will rise as you progress in The Way of the Tiger and may change throughout the adventure.

KICK

The kick and the Kick Modifier work exactly as the punch, except that when you roll the dice to determine the damage you inflict, add 2 to the dice – a kick is more amazing than a punch.

THROW

The throw and Throw Modifier work as the punch. However, if you are successful, no damage is done to your attacker, but you will be allowed another attack, a punch or kick, and it will be much easier to strike a thrown opponent. If you are successful with this, your follow up attack, add 2 to the damage you inflict.

THE NINJA'S ENDURANCE

You begin the game with 20 points of Endurance. Keep a running total of your Endurance score on your Character Sheet. It will probably be the category that will change most as you are wounded, healed etc. When you reach 0 Endurance or less, you are dead and your adventure ends.

THE BLOCK

As a Ninja, a master of Taijutsu, you have the ability to block or parry incoming blows with various parts of your body, often your forearms. For this purpose, thin lightweight iron rods have been sewn into your sleeves enabling you to block even swords and other weapons. During combat, if you have been hit, you may try to block the blow and take no damage. Roll two dice. If the score is less than your Defence given in that combat, you have successfully blocked the blow, and take no damage. If your score is equal to or greater than your Defence, you take damage in the normal way. In any case, because you have taken the time to block, your next attack is less effectual, as your opponent has had more time to react. Whether your block is successful or not, subtract 2 from your Punch, Kick and Throw Modifier for your next attack only. Remember, you can only block blows.

INNER FORCE

Through meditation and rigorous training you have mastered the ability to unleash spiritual or Inner power through your body in the same way as the karate experts of today break blocks of wood and bricks. In any combat, before you roll the dice to determine if you will hit or miss an opponent, you may choose to use Inner Force. If you do, deduct one point from your Inner Force score. This is used up whether or not you succeed in striking your opponent. If you are successful, however, double the score you roll when determining the amount of damage you inflict. When your Inner Force is reduced to 0, you may no longer use Inner Force. So use it wisely! You begin the game with 5 points of Inner Force.

FATE

Luck plays its part and the goddess Fate has great

power on the world of Orb. Whenever you are asked to make a Fate Roll, roll two dice and add or subtract your Fate Modifier. If the score is 7–12, you are lucky and Fate has smiled on you. If the score is 2–6, you are unlucky and Fate has turned her back on you. You begin your adventure with a Fate Modifier of 0.

THE SKILLS OF THE WAY OF THE TIGER

You have been trained in ninjitsu all of your life. Your senses of smell, sight and hearing have been honed to almost superhuman effectiveness. You are well versed in woodcraft, able to track like a bloodhound, and to cover your own tracks. Your knowledge of plants and herb lore enables you to live off the land. You are at the peak of physical fitness, able to run up to 50 miles a day and swim like a fish. Your training included horsemanship, a little ventriloquism, meditation, the ability to hold yourself absolutely still for hours on end, perfecting your balance, and 'The Seven Ways of Going' or disguise. The latter skill involves comprehensive training so that you can perform as a minstrel, for instance, if this disguise is used. However, a major part of this training has been stealth, hiding in shadows, moving silently, and, to breathe as quietly as possible, enabling you to move about unseen and unheard. You begin the game with these skills.

There are nine other skills. One of these, Shuriken-jitsu, is always taught to a Ninja in training. This you must take, but you may then choose three other skills from the remaining eight, and note them down on your Character Sheet.

SHURIKENJITSU

You begin the adventure with five 'Shuriken'. The type you specialise in are 'throwing stars', small razor sharp star shaped disks of metal. You can throw these up to a range of about 30 feet with devastating effect. If you throw a Shuriken, you will be given a Defence number for your target. Roll two dice, and if the score is higher than the Defence number, you will have hit your target. If this is the case, roll one die. The score is the amount of damage the Shuriken does. Subtract it from your target's Endurance. You may find yourself in a position where you are unable to retrieve a Shuriken once you have thrown it. Keep a running total in the box provided on your Character Sheet, crossing off a Shuriken each time you lose one. If you have none left, you can no longer use this skill.

ARROW CUTTING

Requiring excellent muscular co-ordination, hand and eye judgement and reflexes, this skill will enable you to knock aside, or even catch, missiles such as arrows or spears.

ACROBATICS

The ability to leap and jump using flips, cartwheels etc. like a tumbler or gymnast.

IMMUNITY TO POISONS

This involves taking small doses of virulent poisons over long periods of time, slowly building up the body's resistance. This enables the Ninja to survive most poison attempts.

FEIGNING DEATH

Requiring long and arduous training, a Ninja with this ability is able to slow down his heart rate and metabolism through will power alone, thus appearing to be dead.

ESCAPOLOGY

A Ninja with this skill is able to dislocate the joints of the body and to maximise the body's suppleness, allowing movement through small spaces, and escape from bonds and chains by slipping out of them.

POISON NEEDLES

Sometimes known as spitting Needles, a Ninja with this skill can place small darts, coated with a powerful poison that acts in the blood stream, onto his tongue. By curling the tongue into an 'O' shape and spitting or blowing, the dart can be propelled up to an effective range of about 15 feet. A useful surprise attack, the source of which is not always perceptible.

PICKING LOCKS, DETECTING AND DISARMING TRAPS

The ability to open locked doors, chests etc. A Ninja with this skill would carry various lockpicks in the pockets of his costume, including a small crowbar or jemmy. You are also trained to notice traps and to use the lock-picking tools to disarm them.

CLIMBING

Comprehensive training in the use of a Grappling

Hook and hand and foot clamps, or Cat's Claws. The padded four-pronged hook has 40 feet of rope attached to it. Used to hook over walls, niches etc., allowing the Ninja to pull himself up the rope. The Cat's Claws are spiked clamps, worn over the palm of the hand and the instep of the feet, enabling the Ninja to imbed his Claws into a wall and climb straight up like a fly, and even to crawl across ceilings.

NINJA TOOLS

As well as any equipment you may take depending on your skills, as a Ninja you will have certain tools with you from the beginning. These are:

THE NINJA COSTUME

During the day you would normally be disguised as a traveller, beggar or suchlike. At night when on a mission, you would wear costume. This consists of a few pieces of black cloth. One piece is worn as a jacket covering the chest and arms, two others are wound around each leg and held in at the waist. Finally, a long piece of cloth is wrapped around the head, leaving only the eyes exposed. The reverse side of the costume can be white, for travel on snowy ground or green, for travel in woods or grasslands.

IRON SLEEVES

Sewn into the sleeves of your costume, are four thin strips of iron, the length of your forearm. These allow you to parry or block blows from swords and other cutting weapons.

BREATHING TUBE

Made from bamboo, this can be used as a snorkel allowing you to remain under water for long periods of time. It can also be used as a blow-pipe in conjunction with the Poison Needles skill, for added range.

GAROTTE

A specialised killing tool of the Ninja, this is a length of wire used to assassinate enemies by strangulation.

FLASH POWDER

This powder, when thrown in any source of flame, causes a blinding flash. You have enough for one use only.

FLINT AND TINDER

Used for making fires.

SPIDERFISH

Salted and cured, this highly venomous fish is used as a source for the deadly poison used in conjunction with the Poison Needles skill, and as a useful way of removing any guardian beasts.

THE BLOOD OF NIL

You also carry one dose of the most virulent poison known on Orb. This venom is extremely difficult and very dangerous to collect for it is taken from the barb of a scorpion son of the God, Nil, Mouth of the Void.

With these skills and weapons at your disposal you are now a Ninja warrior and ready to take the first step in **The Way of the Tiger**.

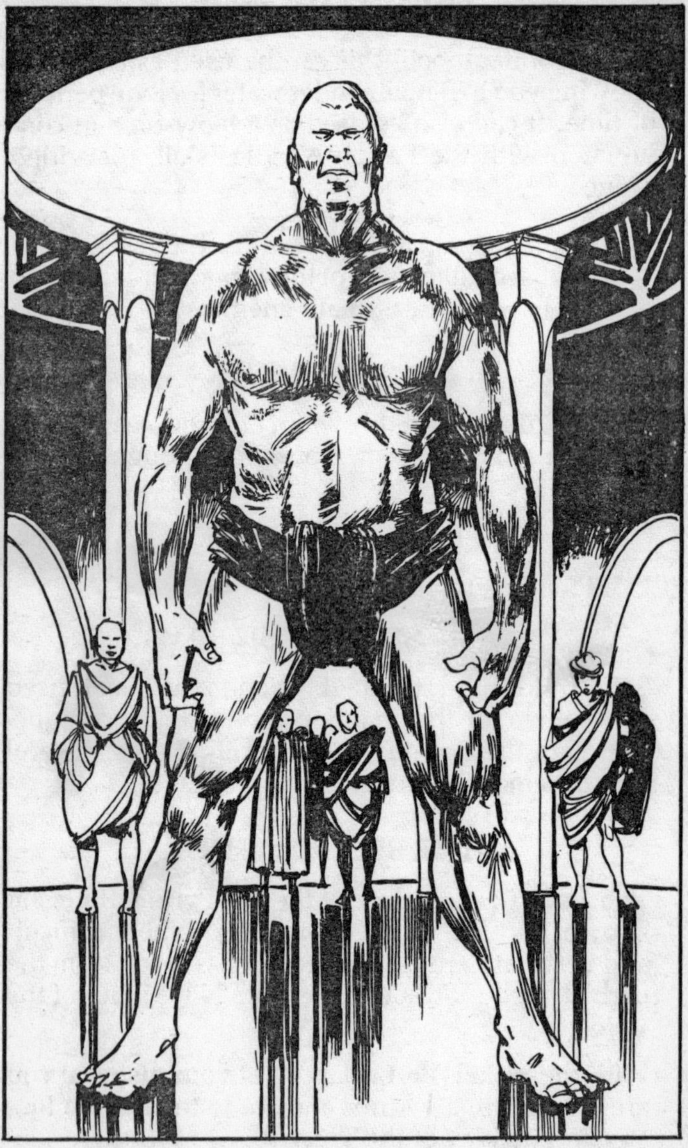

1

The dawn rays of the sun greet you as you begin your preparations for the time of trial. Today you will become the youngest ever to challenge for the title of Grandmaster of the Five Winds. When your foster father, Naijishi, was murdered by Yaemon, the second Grandmaster stepped into his place. Now, many seasons later another of the Grandmasters has died and the position is open once more for there must always be five who lead the order. You have been invited to challenge for it because of your consummate mastery of the Way of the Tiger.

At the appointed hour you walk, alone, across the sands to the Temple of the Rock. It is a huge pillared hall built into the side of an enormous boulder of red granite brought to rest on the Island of Tranquil Dreams by the ice floes of the age of snow, which carved out the Great Valley Reaches of the far north. As you approach the Temple, you see that the monks and a large number of villagers have assembled to watch the combat between you and the other challenger, Gorobei.

Like you, Gorobei is an Initiate of the Inner Circle, a devout worshipper of Kwon and a capable fighter. He is older, heavier and stronger than you and has been unsuccessful in one previous challenge, but he is a skilful wrestler. You walk into the Temple and bow to the Grandmaster of the Dawn, a man who looks younger than his fifty years, slim and taut with piercing dark eyes. Beside you, Gorobei also bows, his face a mask showing no emotion. He is clad only in a loin cloth and his rippling muscles gleam with an oil that will make it difficult to keep a grip on him. You must defeat him in unarmed combat in order to be allowed to undertake the spiritual test which will show whether you are ready to become a Grandmaster. Gorobei turns to you and bows and you return the courtesy. The Grandmaster of the Dawn reminds you that this is not a fight to the death and you may not use Inner Force. He signals for you to begin. Gorobei advances warily across the polished granite floor, his big hands ready to grapple you. Will you:

Feint a punch and then use the Leaping Tiger kick (turn to **17**)?

Pretend to grapple but instead use the Cobra Strike jab (turn to **35**)?

Raise your foot as if to kick but side-step and use the Whirlpool throw (turn to **61**)?

Or, if you are an Acrobat, you may wish to somersault to Gorobei's side before attacking (turn to **80**).

2

The guard walking the rounds of the Inner Bailey does not notice as, with the faintest scraping you force an entry at the window of a store-room. The room opens out onto a spiral staircase which is lit with torches fixed in brackets on the outside wall. Halfway up your keen sight notices a network of fine threads stretched across the staircase and connected to wires which disappear through holes in the inner wall. You stand on your hands and 'walk' up the staircase, feeling for the near invisible threads as you go and straining your ears for the slightest sound. At last you are past them. Turn to **399**.

3

The hook catches the castle wall and you leap towards the far side of the moat. You hit the water with a splash and begin pulling yourself up to the wall as fast as you can. The water boils around you as the Floating Mouths streak towards their prey and two are still fixed to you as you pull yourself out. Lose 3 Endurance as they tear at your flesh. If you are still alive, you sweep them away and, standing up, look around. The Dark Elf is nowhere to be seen, lost in the swamp, and the knight lies spreadeagled on the sand but the man in blue and gold robes is floating across the moat on a small ice floe. Turn to **372**.

4

The priests rush to the edge of the river and one of them catches sight of you and points. They begin to throw off their chainmail. Are you skilful with Poison Needle Darts? If you are and would like to use one, turn to **419**. If you are not or would, in any case, rather swim powerfully away upstream, turn to **12**.

5

You lie in the murk of the swamp and the Troll stench washes over you as it bends down and picks you up in its claws. Lose 2 Endurance for its rough handling as it prepares to eat you. If you are still alive, as you near its gaping maw, you smash your iron sleeves into its face. You see the black blood spurting from its eye begin to dwindle to a trickle as the squashed eye remoulds itself. But it drops you in surprise and you flee as fast as you can. Turn to **14**.

6

You pass through the archway of purple-black glass and on into the city of Doomover itself. You cannot remember ever having seen so many buildings, solid and tall, their roofs of sloping slates, not thatch, and there are shops everywhere, selling fish, wine, grain and there is even a slave market. Near the Obsidian Gate a town-crier begins to ring his bell. He is dressed in orange and green to attract attention, and he begins to shout loudly about a brave adventurer who lived in Doomover who has reaped rich rewards and found a secret way into the death-city of Mortavalon, having entered a cave in the hills which encircle that city. Next he proclaims loudly that the army is paying well for recruits, that there is no war but men are needed for manoeuvres on the Plain of Feet. There are rows of barracks not far from the harbour. Do you:

Decide to enlist in the army to see what information you can gain? Turn to **16**.

Ignore the town crier and walk on through the city? Turn to **408**.

7

You spend the next day in lonely vigil, but no one leaves the castle. It is still a tenday before the moon will turn red at the conjunction of the planets and you can see preparations begin in the outer bailey. Yaemon, Honoric and Manse the Deathmage will set out for the Pillars of Change on the morrow. Your prayers to Kwon for a stormy moonless night are answered and you decide that on this night you will complete your mission or die honourably in the attempt. The wind and the rain and the darkness will make it possible for you to pass into the castle as if invisible. You prepare yourself in silent meditation, and don your Ninja costume before staring up into the darkness until your night vision is as acute as an owl's. If you have the skill of Climbing and wish to scale the castle wall, turn to **392**. Otherwise, you may raise the grille outside the moat and drop to the tunnel below. In this case, turn to **402**.

8

The Barbarian tenses as you place the needle on your rolled tongue and spit it out in one fluid motion. The needle pierces his cheek. He has an iron constitution and although a look of agony twists his features, his system overcomes the virulent poison. You may note that he has lost 4 Endurance. As you pause in astonishment, he strikes at you and his sword cleaves the air towards your shoulder. Your Defence against his blow is 8 as you try to bring your left forearm up to sweep aside the blade. If he hits you, his sword will do 1 Die + 1 damage. If you survive you may use the Cobra Strike (turn to **377**), the Winged Horse (turn to **302**) or the Dragon's Tail (turn to **318**).

9

Although the hooded cobra can strike faster than the eye can see, you are faster still. You grab its neck in one hand and slice off its head with a Shuriken held in the other. Manse is on his back but he can still cast spells and his Eldritch words ring in your brain as the force of his magic is again brought to bear. He clenches his fist and it is as if iron bars were pressing on you from all sides. His pallid face quivers with effort as he clenches the fist ever tighter until your ribcage collapses. He opens his hand and you fall lifeless to the floor. You have failed your mission.

10

He looks at you and nods, apparently satisfied. You sleep the night in the strange monk's cave. He has few possessions and says he has not seen another human being in years, except in sleep. It seems he feeds on air for he has nothing to offer you other than cool and refreshing mountain rain-water. In the morning he claims that he has, somehow, seen Yaemon, Grandmaster of Flame, journeying north with Honoric, servant of Vasch-Ro, Marshal of the Legion of the Sword of Doom, from the city of Doomover.

'And they journey to meet a third,' he says, 'Manse the Deathmage, who reverences Nemesis. A most powerful and evil sorcerer. This unholy alliance must be stopped. Of all the evil gods, only the followers of Vile, Vasch-Ro and Nemesis have the discipline to act in alliance. Nemesis is the greatest of the evil gods. Never before have three such powerful and evil men trusted each other.'

'It is the conjunction of the planets,' you reply. Togawa pulls a bag of herbs from a crack in the rock.

'These have healing virtue,' he says. You take them and may use them at any time when you are not being attacked to restore up to 8 Endurance points, once only. You thank him and are about to ask him if he will accompany you when he lies down on the cave floor and goes to sleep. Sensing that there is no further help to be gained, you begin the climb down Mount Gwalodrun to the pass below. A day later you enter the foothills of Fortune Pass. Turn to **70**.

11

The Shuriken only wounds the first guard and he

cries the alarm. You see magical lights appearing around the castle like Will-O'-the-Wisps and decide to climb back down the tower, cross the moat once more and try to enter the castle through the grille that leads to an underground tunnel. Turn to 398.

12
You swim upstream but as you go they begin chanting again, and as their spell takes effect you find you cannot move your limbs. You float gently downstream, into their welcoming arms and they bind you securely. If you have a Ring they take it from you, cross it off your Character Sheet. Are you a skilled Escapologist? If you are, turn to 21. If you are not, turn to 37.

13
You try to leap up and lock your legs around the Cobra Man's neck as he strikes, to twist and throw him to the ground, but his speed still surprises you.

COBRA MAN
Defence against throw: 7
Endurance: 10

If you have thrown the Cobra Man you may now either attack using the Tiger's Paw chop (turn to 42) or the Winged Horse kick (turn to 25), adding 2 to your Kick or Punch Modifier for this attack only. If you have failed to throw the Cobra Man turn to 412.

14
In your haste you stray perilously close to the edge of the track. The treacherous swamp is all around you, hidden in the mist. Make a Fate Roll. If Fate smiles on you, turn to 417. If Fate turns her back on you, turn to 404.

15

You take your leave of the soldier and walk quickly away from the castle. Turn to **145**.

16

You walk to the barracks and join a queue of people, some young and fit, others older, looking a little down on their luck. You are chosen with a few of the others to demonstrate your skill with the sword, which you manage adequately but not well, never having been trained in sword play. You are grouped together and given drill practice for some hours before being marched to your night barracks. You manage to discover that the Legion of the Sword of Doom is going to attack the people of the Spires of Foreshadowing but that there is plenty of time to be trained for battle, because its leader, Honoric, has left the city and journeyed north. As you all settle down to sleep, they begin to talk of pillaging the Spires and the loot that they will bring home. The barracks are guarded in case any of the new recruits think better of joining up but you decide that there is nothing more of interest here and try to desert in the quiet hours before dawn. You wrap your black Ninja headgear around your head until only the slits of your eyes are visible and don your black costume.

If you have the skill of Climbing and would like to leave the barracks from the roof, turn to **75**. Otherwise, you decide to creep up behind the guard whilst the others sleep. Turn to **86**.

17

You step forward as if to punch, then, leaping in the air you lash the ball of your foot towards Gorobei's head with a speed that defies belief. Gorobei, although not quick, knows your style of combat.

GOROBEI
Defence against kick: 6
Endurance: 14
Damage: 1 Die

If you have defeated Gorobei turn to **110**.

If Gorobei is still conscious he attacks you. Your defence against Gorobei's Cobra Strike is 7.

If Gorobei has defeated you turn to **95**.

Otherwise, will you feint and punch (turn to **35**), feint and throw (turn to **61**) or kick again (return to the top of this paragraph)?

18

There is the merest death rattle as the wire dissects his windpipe and you lower his body gently to the floor, before re-fixing the grappling hook and sliding down to the grass of the Inner Bailey which surrounds the Great Keep. Will you climb to the top of the Keep (turn to **174**) or climb the Keep up to the first row of windows and force an entry there (turn to **2**)?

19

The Aquamarin's huge oars are each manned by

two. At your side a rower, until recently free but now roped by the reavers to the oar shaft, stares blankly at you. You can tell by the white scars on his back that he is one of the two who has been in slave galleys before. His upper body is huge, his chest unnaturally deep and his legs squat and tapering to small feet, giving him the appearance of a toad. He tells you that he had been enslaved as a boy and knows no other life than that of the oar deck. He groans quietly at the savage twist of Fate that has befallen him and tells you that he was the only one on his last slave ship to live longer than a year. The buccaneers appoint an Overseer and two whip hands to patrol the Aquamarin's oar deck. It seems they are going to sell her and her crew at some lawless port. Are you an Escapologist? If you are, turn to **126**. If you are not, turn to **115**.

20

'Look around you,' says Togawa, 'is this my home?' You stare at him, nonplussed. 'No,' he goes on, 'my home is my body and your home is your body.' Turn to **10**.

21

The priests camp in the hills which encircle Mortavalon, near a cave-mouth, overhung with rock. After they have eaten round a small fire, two of them walk over to where you lie. Instead of giving you food they tell you that they are taking you back to the dungeons under the cathedral to Vasch-Ro, in Doomover, where you will rot. Intrigued you ask them why they are taking you there instead of to their own temple at Mortavalon.

'Because Manse the Deathmage, a servant of

Nemesis and the most powerful sorcerer of them all, is journeying north to meet Honoric and Yaemon, he of the order of the Scarlet Mantis, to work a great magic which will plunge the world into darkness and bring nearer the day when we, the followers of Nemesis, will rule everything on Orb.'

'Yaemon will betray him,' you say.

They laugh and reply that the Deathmage knows the thoughts of all men and can see them plotting from afar. With that they leave you, preparing themselves for sleep. For some hours you wrestle with your bonds, loosening them until you can hook your thumbs inside the chafing ropes. At last you are free and you decide to creep into the cave, lest they use spells to snare you once again. Turn to **275**.

22

The guard hesitates, then says, 'Wait here, while I fetch the necessary papers. You will need a pass.' With that he signals another soldier to take over and walks under the portcullis into the castle bailey. Do you await his return (turn to **31**) or leave in case he has gone to prepare a trap (turn to **15**)?

23

The Barbarian's voice rises to a shriek of battle lust as he swipes at you, berserk. He cares nothing for your attacks so long as his sword tastes your blood. Subtract one from any damage you do to him. He cuts his sword down towards your head, but you sidestep to the right, twist and lash your left foot towards his face as his sword whistles down past your back.

OLVAR THE BARBARIAN
Defence against Winged Horse: 7
Endurance: 18
Damage: 1 Die + 1

If you have defeated Olvar, turn to **47**. If he still lives, he swings his sword from right to left through the point where you are standing. Your Defence is 8 as you hop backwards.

If you are still alive you may punch (turn to **92**), throw (turn to **39**) or kick again (return to the top of this paragraph).

24

As his foot nears your head, you try and drive the palm of your right hand up onto his ankle and force his leg over your head, but you have misjudged it, and your arm cleaves the air past his leg. His foot slams into your face. The power of his Inner Force is stunning and blood spurts from your shattered nose and mangled lips. Lose 10 Endurance. If you are still alive, the force of the blow sends you flying backwards. Using all of your will power, you suppress the pain and flip backwards onto your feet, as Yaemon runs at you to attack again. You have no time to kick, but you can try to punch (turn to **155**) or throw him (turn to **68**).

25

The Cobra Man's strike is as fast as your own as you turn sideways on and drive your heel towards his chest.

COBRA MAN
Defence against kick: 7
Endurance: 10

If you have killed the Cobra Man, turn to **394**. If your kick has missed, he strikes home (turn to **412**). Otherwise will you use the Tiger's Paw chop (turn to **42**), try the Teeth of the Tiger throw (turn to **13**) or kick again (return to the top of this paragraph)?

26

By midday of the next day, the Aquamarin has left the islands behind and ahead of you looms the Greater Continent. You turn north and hug the rocky coast for some days; you may restore up to ten points of lost Endurance as you rest, gliding over the still calm seas. It begins to rain slightly on the next day, as you follow the shore of a vast bay. Glaivas comes to talk to you and points to a large estuary where the Greybones empties into the sea. He tells you that his home city, Tor, lies up river. You ask him whether there is a temple to Kwon there and he shakes his head but freely tells you that his goddess is the Allmother, Preserver of Life. You ask him of the cities which lie beyond Tor on the Greybones river but a look of pain crosses his face.

'Let me tell you, instead, of Doomover, for that is our port of call,' he says. 'It is one of the largest cities in the Manmarch, perhaps four hundred thousand souls, and it is ruled by the Legion of the Sword of Doom. Most spit when they hear the name but they are one of the best armies on Orb. They worship the Wargod, Vasch-Ro, He who sows for the Reaper, and they spread fear about them in battle. There are temples to other gods but the Cathedral to the Wargod overshadows them all. The Marshal of the Legion of the Sword of Doom is Honoric, a blackheart who has never been defeated in combat. It is said that he once slew a storm giant, single handed. He is without doubt a peerless swordsman. The order of the Scarlet Mantis has a temple there too. They send their acolytes to the Far Snows for training, where they become used to hardship of all kinds. Yaemon is the greatest warrior they have ever had to lead them. They use the cross of Avatar, the Supreme Principle of Good as a symbol, but with a serpent twining round it. In this way you may know one if you see one.'

On the next day, you sight the fortified harbour walls of Doomover and two long blackwood ships dart out to meet you. They fly the flag of the Barbican, the Doomover navy. As they approach, a tall man in black ringed mail orders you to heave to. The captain obeys and the sails are slackened. He answers various questions but when the naval commander asks what business he has at Doomover, he looks nervously at Glaivas, licking his lips. Glaivas answers for him, saying that he has come to sell galley slaves.

The commander grins, 'I was going to confiscate your ship but as you bring men we have need of, you may pass through the Barbican.' With that you are allowed on your way.

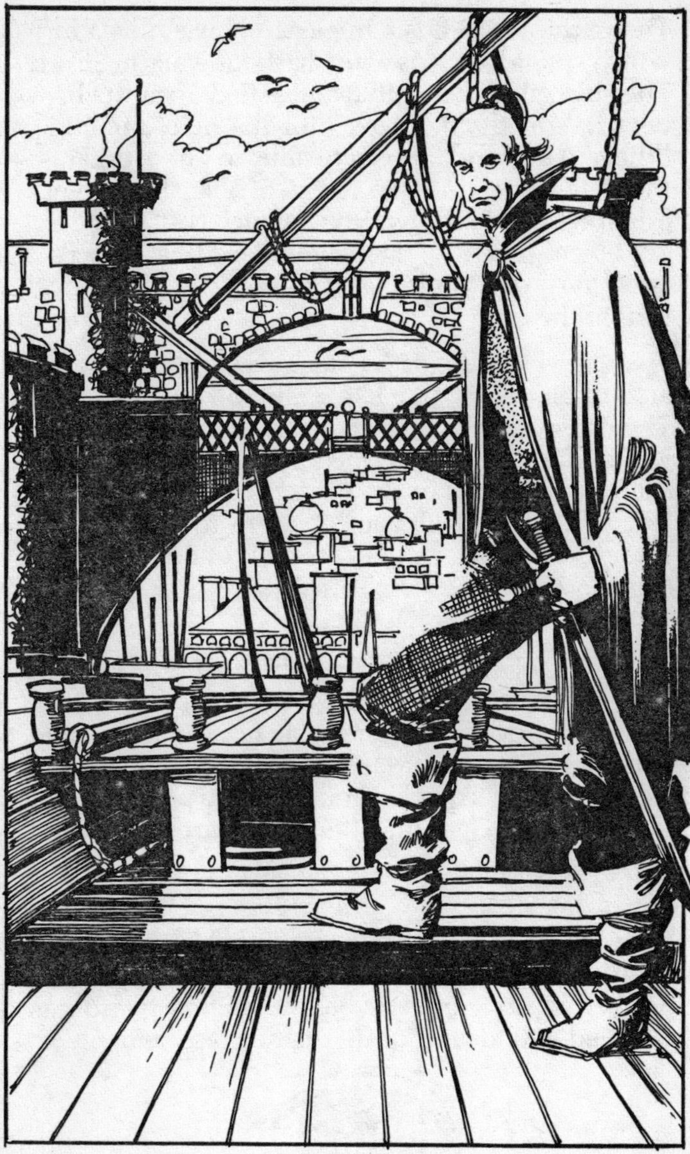

The Barbican itself is a huge gatehouse, like a fort, which spans the ends of the harbour walls in an arc. The ship glides beneath it and is tied up at the busy wharf. You thank Glaivas for his help and jump lithely to the land. He is returning to Tor to organise the defence against the forces of Vile should your mission fail. He throws you a pouch containing ten gold pieces, saying, 'Here, you need this. May Fate smile on you, Ninja.' You pocket the pouch and turn to the city.

Two gates stand side by side. The larger is a huge arch of black obsidian like a rainbow of dark glass. The other, much smaller, consists of two pairs of white marble pillars topped by a portico on which the words 'Portal of the Gods' are written in gold leaf. Which gate will you choose to go through, the Obsidian Gate (turn to **6**) or the Portal of the Gods (turn to **208**)?

27

The girl looks at you scornfully, as if you were in some way unworthy. The old man screams at you, 'May Fate never smile on you again.' He has cursed you. Subtract one from your Fate Modifier. You leave the chapel quickly and decide to pass through the Obsidian Gate into the main part of the city. Turn to **6**.

28

He catches the wire which bites into his mail gauntlet and shouts the alarm. You kill him quickly but not before the crossbow bolt of another guard has tumbled you to your death on the grass below.

29
You leap above the now huge gem which tumbles down the staircase behind you and lash out at the Deathmage with a Winged Horse kick before you land. He is hurled to the floor like a rag doll. As he falls he throws down his snake-staff which transforms into a living cobra, its hood spread as it slithers towards you, ready to strike. Will you ignore it and leap onto the Deathmage to try to finish him off (turn to 400) or try to grab the snake's neck before it can strike (turn to 9)?

30
A huge Troll, its warted skin green and slimy, bursts out of the mist and pulls up in front of you. You kick and punch it for all you are worth but as fast as you inflict wounds they heal again, magically, the torn flesh crawling across the bones to re-knit together, leaving only purple scars. The Troll claws you and you lose 4 Endurance. If you are still alive, it seems that you will lose this battle. Will you turn and flee as fast as you can (turn to 14) or, if you have the skill, Feign Death (turn to 5)?

31
You wait for the guard to reappear when there is a faint grating noise behind you. You spin in time to see Honoric and Manse the Deathmage stepping out from a secret doorway and go for a throwing star, but Manse casts a spell and your body is gripped by a trembling palsy. You are powerless to resist as Honoric deftly cleaves your head from your shoulders with a sword.

32

Togawa nods. 'What are your weapons?' he demands. Will you reply:

'I have no need of weapons.' Turn to **10**.

OR

'My weapons are everything that exists.' Turn to **304**.

33

You leap from the boat, high into the air and arc gracefully towards the far side as the crowd gasp in awe. Make a Fate Roll. If Fate smiles on you, turn to **382**. If Fate turns her back on you, you will fall short, into the moat – turn to **64**.

34

Crash! The Captain's head hits the deck on the way down and his skull is staved in before the waves engulf him. The news spreads quickly through the reavers and they break off the battle, jumping back to the Watery Death and begin fighting in earnest to decide who shall become the new tyrant captain. You dive from the stern castle and swim strongly towards the Aquamarin which is already under way. Your lungs bursting, you catch onto a moving oar at last, and haul yourself up over the side. Turn to **26**.

35

You crouch as if to wrestle with Gorobei who tenses, ready to throw his extra weight against yours, but you jab unexpectedly towards his midriff. Gorobei's reach is long and he is skilled in punching and blocking, though not as fast as you.

GOROBEI
Defence against Punch: 7
Endurance: 14
Damage: 1 Die

If you have defeated Gorobei turn to **110**.

If Gorobei is still conscious, he attacks you. Your Defence against his Tiger's Paw chop is 7.

If Gorobei has reduced your Endurance to 0 or less, turn to **95**.

Or, will you now feint and kick (turn to **17**), feint and throw (turn to **61**) or punch again (return to the top of this paragraph)?

36

The Seer is shuffling towards a porch at the entrance of the small wooden chapel that lies beyond the temple to Béatan the Free. He turns towards you and beckons you inside. The chapel is small and dark but to your surprise it is clean and well kept. Scrolls are neatly stacked in racks along the walls.

The old man calls a girl's name and his acolyte appears, a surprisingly pretty girl of no more than eighty seasons. Whilst you wonder what she is doing with the stooped old man in a chapel that is too small to hold more than twenty people, he produces a long and wicked looking sacrificial knife. In the darkness of the chapel his features look more gaunt and powerful than they did when he raved at the priests. He tells you to lie down on what looks like a small marble tomb with a silver ewer beside it. The young girl reaches to guide you to it. If you trust them and allow her to guide you, turn to **50**. If you decide to take your leave hastily, turn to **27**.

37

Try as you might you cannot loosen your bonds. You overhear the priests talking and it seems that they worship Nemesis, the Supreme Principle of Evil. Somehow word of your exploits in Doomover has travelled ahead of you, but you cannot puzzle out why the priests of Nemesis are in league with the monks of the Scarlet Mantis and the Legion of the Sword of Doom who follow the Wargod Vasch-Ro. They return you to Doomover where you are taken to the dungeons below the cathedral to Vasch-Ro and manacled to the wall. The jailor does not bother to bring you food or water and you are dead within days.

38

Once again you use the grappling hook and skim quickly and soundlessly up the wall. At the top you see a guard who has heard the dull thud of the

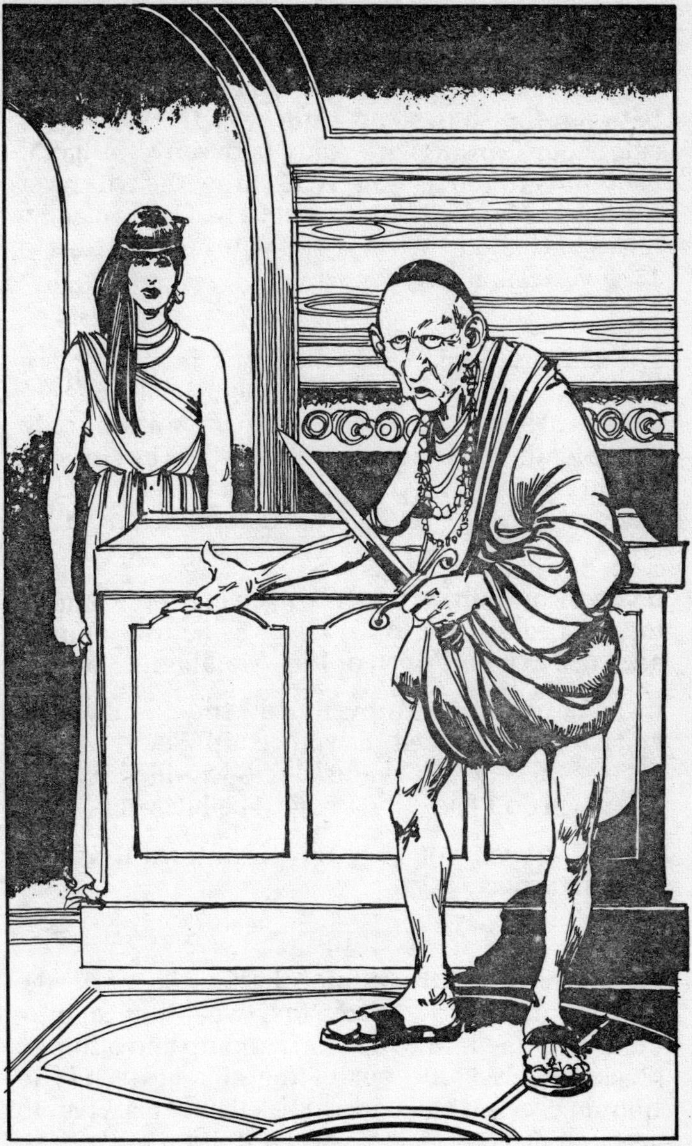

felt-covered hook as it fell atop the wall. You climb sideways from the hook using convenient handholds where the concrete has been washed from between the stones and vault over the wall at his side, your Garotte-wire ready between your teeth. He whirls round as you try to throw the wire over his head. Make an Attack Roll. His Defence as he raises his hand in alarm is 4. If you succeed, turn to **18**. If you fail, turn to **28**.

39

The Barbarian has worked himself into a berserk frenzy of battle lust, cleaving the air with mighty sweeps of his sword, heedless of pain, wanting only your blood. The Dragon's Tail takes him by surprise as you try and sweep his legs from under him. His Defence is only 4 as his sword cuts the air above you.

If you throw him successfully, you may punch (turn to **92**) or kick (turn to **23**) Olvar as he tries to rise, adding 2 to your Punch or Kick Modifier.

If you have failed to throw him, he tries to cut you in half from brow to belly as you get up. Your Defence against this cut as he vents a bloodcurdling roar, is 6. He will do 1 Die + 1 damage if he hits you.

If you survive, you may now kick (turn to **23**) or punch (turn to **92**).

40

Your aim is slightly off and the Shuriken whistle past Yaemon's head. As the first two disappear into the night, Yaemon whips his hand up and adroitly plucks the last one out of the air, and sends it spinning back at you with a quick flick of his wrist. It takes all of your skill to sweep it aside at the last moment with your forearm and it ricochets away with a whine. Yaemon was not expecting you to parry your own Shuriken and you have a moment within which to act. Will you use a Poison Needle, if you know how to (turn to **69**) or close with Yaemon and attack (turn to **89**)?

41

You make no sound and using the Ninja catwalk you cause your tracks to appear as though you were heading in the opposite direction out of the swamp. But the huge beast tracks you by smell alone and the great splashing of its lumbering strides increases pace. Will you throw caution to the wind and run faster (turn to **14**) or stand and fight (turn to **30**)?

42

As the Cobra Man's lidless eyes watch, warily waiting for you to commit yourself, you drive the back of your hand towards the swaying neck, but you will do well to beat the snake man's whip-like strike.

COBRA MAN
Defence against Tiger's Paw chop: 7
Endurance: 10

If you have killed the Cobra Man, turn to **394**. If you have failed to chop his swaying head, turn to **412**. Otherwise will you use the Winged Horse kick (turn to **25**), try the Teeth of the Tiger throw (turn to **13**) or punch again (return to the top of this paragraph)?

43

'Look around you,' says Togawa, 'is this my home?' You stare at him, nonplussed. 'No,' he goes on, 'my home is my body and your home is your body.' Turn to **10**.

44

As you try to run at the priests their spell takes hold and your legs and arms turn to lead. Your body quivers as, with a great effort of will, you struggle a few steps further but they have no trouble in knocking you to the ground and tying you securely. If you have a Ring, they take it from you, cross it off your Character Sheet. Are you a skilled Escapologist? If you are, turn to **21**. If not, turn to **37**.

45

You duck the Captain's swirling morning star, then dodge as he tries to surprise you by driving the heavy gold rings on his left fist into your face. Before you can attack him again a chain net descends upon you and you fall, struggling, to the boards. Two buccaneers had seen you attacking their Captain and being his favourites, they rush to his aid, flinging a chain net from the stairway. They tie you up and drag you back to the Aquamarin where your Ninja tools are taken and you are roped to an oar. Turn to **19**.

46

'We are always ready to help a follower of the Preserver of Life,' says the priest. You ask him if a monk, a follower of Vile, called Yaemon, is in Doomover. The priest tells you that the talk of the town is that Honoric, the Marshal of the Legion of the Sword of Doom, left the city a tenday since, just when his men were expecting him to lead them in battle against the people of the Spires of Foreshadowing. He continues, 'I don't know why he left so suddenly but it must be important.' He pauses.

'But what of Yaemon?' you ask.

'Ah yes, well, the monks of the Scarlet Mantis have

always been on good terms with the reverencers of Vasch-Ro the Wargod. Yaemon went with him on the road to Mortavalon.' He can tell you no more other than that they rode and were alone. You thank him and leave the temple. Do you:

Go through the Obsidian Gate (turn to 6)?
Leave Doomover out of the harbour gate and head for Mortavalon (turn to 65)?

47

The Barbarian falls at last, a mass of broken bones. At the end it seemed that he would fight on for ever but his battle cries will no longer trouble the lands of Orb. Runeweaver's sight has returned and he has been watching the closing rounds of the battle. As soon as Olvar falls dead he darts in and grabs the circlet with the blue jewel from the Barbarian's forehead.

'I'll take this,' he says and draws his sword on you. Will you fight the man you saved from the birdmen, for the circlet (turn to 78), or let him go, take 5 gold pieces from Olvar's body and either head north west out of the pass to the City of Far Snows (turn to 313), or towards the City of Druath Glennan (turn to 219) or turn east through the Trollfens to the City of Ionalbion to take ship across the Sea of the Star (turn to 59)?

48

'You were entertaining the poor for no reward? No wonder I didn't see your act. On you go then,' and he waves you into the castle bailey, a courtyard surrounded by high walls on all sides. Turn to 112.

49

The magical field of force glows, but your throwing

star carries such force that it passes through, knocking Manse to the floor. As he falls he throws down his snake-staff which transforms into a living cobra, its hood spread as it slithers towards you ready to strike. Will you ignore it and leap onto the Deathmage to try to finish him off (turn to **400**) or try to grab the snake's neck before it can strike (turn to **9**)?

50

The girl takes your hand in hers and leads you to the marble slab. The old man explains that he must let some of your blood into the silver chalice if he is to show you the future. He cuts a vein in your arm and the blood pumps into the ewer. You look at him in alarm as he lets it flow until you have lost half a pint and your arm begins to tingle. Subtract 2 from your Endurance. Then he seals the wound with a spell. The girl pours a green potion into the ewer. You feel faint and obey him when he tells you to look at a mirror which hangs on the wall above you. He begins to chant and produces a crystal prism which he holds over the ewer. The blood and potion bubble and the Seer's chanting grows louder. A picture forms in the mirror of two men leaving a city on horseback. The larger is dressed in black plate mail and carries a black shield upon which is emblazoned a silver sword hanging from a silver thread, the Sword of Doom. His face is arrogant and cruel. The other is dressed in the clothes of a martial arts monk, scarlet with a thin black belt. They are riding towards you in silence and the monk's piercing black eyes gaze unwavering, into yours. The Seer informs you that the vision shows Yaemon Grandmaster of Flame, riding with Honoric, Marshal of the Legion of the Sword of Doom, north from Mortavalon. He tells you that they are travelling to the Pillars of Change, each to speak a word which will imprison a god and a goddess in Inferno. Honoric seeks to rule the whole of the Manmarch. You fall into a trance and when you wake up you find yourself outside Doomover, walking on the road to Mortavalon. You wonder what the Seer may have done whilst you were entranced. Has he told anyone of your vision? At any rate, the vision suggested that Honoric and Yaemon were far ahead. You realise that you must travel to Mortavalon to find out where Yaemon and Honoric are. Turn to **65**.

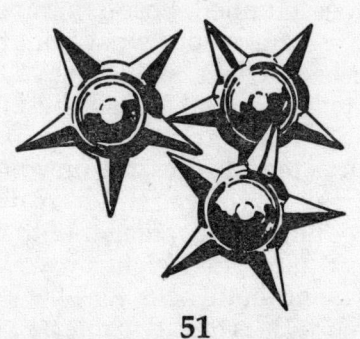

51

With lightning speed your hand flashes through the air three times in rapid succession and three Shuriken fly towards Yaemon. Make a Shuriken Roll. Yaemon's Defence is 6. If you succeed, turn to **378**. If you fail, turn to **40**.

52

You empty the Essence of Firenewt powder on the surface of the moat and it stimulates the bullfrogs to recommence their croaking. Turn to **74**.

53

'Look around you,' says Togawa, 'is this my home?' You stare at him, nonplussed. 'No,' he goes on, 'my

home is my body and your home is your body.'
Turn to **10**.

54

You twist on your left foot, bringing your right ankle in a whipping arc aimed at Yaemon's head. This time he is ready for you and ducks again, under your flailing foot. As you come round to face him, he hops up, and drives his right foot into your groin, followed by his left up into your face in a quick scissor kick. You drop to your back on the floor like a sack of potatoes, stunned. Lose 8 Endurance. If you are still alive, he grabs your wrist from the ground and turns his back to you, straddling your arm with his legs. He twists around and sits beside you, one calf across your neck. You cry out in pain and he begins to exact a terrible pressure on your arm in an attempt to break it. You resist, but realise that the arm-lock gives him the advantage. With remarkable dexterity, you put your weight on your shoulder blades and swing both your feet back over your head at Yaemon. He is forced to release you to block your attack and, as he does so, you whip your feet back and, with the palms of your hands on the ground behind your head, push hard, flipping to your feet, before Yaemon can act. You leap out of range and turn to face him as he rises to his feet. Still somewhat groggy you shake your head to clear it, in time to see Yaemon leap towards you and unleash a flurry of attacks. If you have Acrobatics, turn to **181**. If you have not, you must try to block. Your Defence is 7. If you succeed, turn to **118**. If you fail, turn to **308**.

55

Your last blow sends one of them collapsing backwards towards the river. You have pummelled them all to death. The wagons are nowhere to be seen, but you notice that one of them is wearing an Amulet. The Amulet is a bright crystal set in a gold disk which carries an inscription, as well as magical runes: 'My wearer can withstand the Finger of Death'. You slip the Amulet around your neck; note it down on your Character Sheet. Searching their bodies you find a battered scroll case and, muttering a prayer to Kwon to protect you from curses, you open it. The papyrus inside identifies its bearer as a priest of Nemesis, 'The Supreme Principle of Evil, he who would return all to The Darkness.' It carries a description of you. It was no accident that they attacked you, word has somehow travelled ahead of you for their temple to Nemesis is in Mortavalon. You walk on into the hills which encircle Mortavalon, puzzling as to who could have contacted the temple to Nemesis about you and why, until, turning a bend in the hills, you notice a cave overhung by rock in the hillside above you. Will you continue along the road to Mortavalon (turn to 283) or enter the cave (turn to 275)?

56

He asks you to give the sign of the many ways to freedom and you cannot. He prepares to cast a spell, but you beg his pardon and, saying that you will seek help elsewhere, quickly leave the temple. The Seer is nowhere to be seen so you walk out of the Sanctuary and through the Obsidian Gate. Turn to 6.

57

You hurl your grappling hook and rope at the castle wall. Make a Fate Roll. If Fate smiles on you, turn to 3. If Fate turns her back on you, the hook misses and you sink into the water before you can retrieve it. In this case, turn to **64**.

58

The buccaneer Captain falls to the planks, dead. Two of his men are on the stairway behind you but seeing that you have killed the man they feared single-handed, they back away, calling the news to the other reavers. The pirates abandon the Aquamarin, returning to the Watery Grave, and begin fighting in earnest to decide who shall become the new tyrant captain.

You dive from the stern castle into the sea and swim strongly towards the Aquamarin, which is already under way. Your lungs bursting, you catch onto a moving oar at last, and haul yourself up over the side. Turn to **26**.

59

You trot steadily on for two days, keeping the saw-toothed Mountains of Vision on your right before coming to a dank land of mists, the Trollfens. They are an enormous expanse of marshland and in the mist you have no way of knowing how long it would take to skirt them to the south. You decide to continue across them, following the tracks made by a small animal. As you trudge across the wet ground the mist grows deeper and then a huge dark shape looms towards you, the slopping of its great feet in the mud deadened by the mist. It stops and sniffs loudly. Will you move carefully but quickly onwards (turn to **41**) or stand and wait for it to find you (turn to **30**)?

60

The throwing star hangs in the air before him,

locked in his magical field of force which glows as it absorbs the impact. As you leap to the attack his spell is finished and flame wells up within you. Smoke pours from your mouth and nose as your lungs and other internal organs catch fire. The Deathmage has cast the spell of The Inner Fire upon you, known only to the most powerful of evil sorcerers and you have been cremated from within.

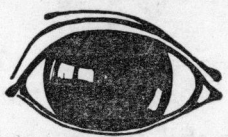

61

You raise your foot as if to kick Gorobei in the chest but spin to his side instead and take hold of his arm to throw him over your hip. You rapidly learn your mistake, however, as your grip slides on the oil which covers him and he uses his skill as a wrestler to grab you and lock your arm behind your back whilst he grips you around the throat. His strength is enormous. You try to somersault backwards over him and break the grip but he is ready for you and pins you to the floor before delivering a heavy blow. Turn to **95**.

62

The guard hesitates, then says, 'Wait here while I fetch the necessary papers. You will need a pass.' With that he signals another soldier to take over and walks under the portcullis into the castle bailey. Do you await his return (turn to **31**) or leave in case he has gone to prepare a trap (turn to **15**)?

63

You leap feet first at one of the priests, trying to

wrap your feet around his head, before twisting to throw him to the ground. You may choose which one to attack.

	1st PRIEST	2nd PRIEST	3rd PRIEST
Defence against Teeth of the Tiger	4	5	5
Endurance	12	14	13
Damage	1 Die +1	1 Die +1	1 Die +1

If you are successful, you try to use the Tiger's Paw chop on the prone priest, who desperately tries to roll aside. His Defence is 3, and if you hit him, add 2 to the Damage Roll. If you kill him with the Tiger's Paw, and he was the last priest alive turn to **55**. If he is still alive or you failed to throw him at all, any of the priests left alive try to bludgeon you with their maces. If 3 are alive, your Defence is 7. If 2 are alive, your Defence is 8, and if only one is left, your Defence is 9. You may block only one of the attacks. If you survive, you may now use the Cobra Strike punch (turn to **82**), or the Forked Lightning kick (turn to **71**).

64

As soon as you hit the water it seems to boil around you as the Floating Mouths race to latch onto their prey. You struggle, but it is useless. Within a minute your skeleton has been stripped bare of its flesh. Your adventure ends here.

65

As you leave the forbidding towered walls of Doomover behind, the sun climbs in the sky, ripening the corn and barley which rustles in the breeze. The fields do not stretch for far and you are soon on the edge of a low plain, the Plain of Feet, on which several thousand of the Legion of the Sword of Doom, smart and efficient, are practising for the forthcoming war. The smooth plain gradually gives way to a wilderness of trees and vines. Will you continue along the road to Mortavalon (turn to **212**) or strike north of the road, into the wilderness (turn to **235**)?

66

The cave is bare. Togawa squats, cross-legged on the floor and you follow suit. He compliments you on your skill in the Way of the Tiger, but recognising that he is more accomplished than you, you compliment him in turn, commenting on the kick which killed the Rock Hulk. He offers to show it to you. He calls it Kwon's Flail and it is more powerful even than the kicks which you use. Note it on your Character Sheet as a new kick you have learnt. You may add + 1 to your Kick Modifier for the advice which Togawa gives. You tell him that you are from the Island of Tranquil Dreams, and of your mission, asking for his help. He surprises you by asking this question. 'Where is your home?'

Do you answer

'I have no home.' Turn to **20**.
'My home is my body.' Turn to **32**.
'As I said, the Island of Tranquil Dreams.' Turn to **43**.
'I believe in Kwon, the world is my home.' Turn to **53**.

67

Make a note of how many times you try to attack the Reaver. Before the morning star makes contact you snap your leg upwards, driving the ball of your foot at the Captain's face.

BUCCANEER CAPTAIN
Defence against Leaping Tiger: 6
Endurance: 12
Damage: 1 Die + 2

If you have defeated the Captain, turn to **58**.

If he is still alive after four attacks, turn to **45**.

Otherwise, he attacks you with his morning star. Your Defence against the spiked ball and chain is 7.

If you are still alive, you may now try the Teeth of the Tiger throw (turn to **87**), a Cobra Strike (turn to **77**) or kick again (return to the top of this paragraph).

68

He is much too quick for you to use the Teeth of the Tiger throw, but will you try to use the Whirlpool throw as he runs in (turn to **367**) or the Dragon's Tail throw (turn to **319**)? You must decide now whether or not to use Inner Force if you have any left.

69

As fast as you are able, you place a needle on your tongue as you somersault forwards through the air to bring yourself within range. As you land on your feet, you spit hard and the needle arrows towards Yaemon. He makes no attempt to move, but then, to your amazement, he blows the small dart aside, inches from his face. Then he crouches and leaps high into the air towards you, his left leg extended in a flying Winged Horse kick aimed at your head. He gives a great shout and you realise he is using Inner Force. If you have Acrobatics, turn to **350**. If not, you have no option but to try and block the kick. Your Defence is 8. If you succeed, turn to **411**. If you fail, turn to **24**.

70

The youthful river Fortune pours down a narrow valley which winds like a snake between the escarpments of the Mountains of Vision. The air becomes cooler as you climb and snow begins to fall. You turn your costume inside out, so that the white lining will camouflage you in the snow. You sleep well in the pass, despite the cold, and may restore up to 4 points of Endurance. On the second day you hear a cry from around an escarpment and you move on stealthily to look. A warrior holds his sword aloft as a small group of Arocs, bird-men, attack. As you watch, a bolt of green light speeds from his sword, felling one of the Arocs. Will you help the warrior, who is hard-pressed (turn to **271**), or hide in the snow until the Arocs leave (turn to **284**).

71

You try to drive the heel of your foot into the groin of one of the priests and then whip it up to his face. You may choose which one you wish to attack.

	1st PRIEST	2nd PRIEST	3rd PRIEST
Defence against Forked Lightning Strike	4	5	5
Endurance	12	14	13
Damage	1 Die + 1	1 Die + 1	1 Die + 1

If you have defeated them, turn to **55**. If any are left alive, they attack you with their maces. Each has an individual Attack. If there are 3 of them, your Defence is 7. If there are 2 of them, your Defence is 8. If there is only one of them, your Defence is 9. You may only block one of their attacks. If you survive their attack, you may try the Teeth of the Tiger throw (turn to **63**), the Cobra Strike (turn to **82**) or kick again (return to the top of this paragraph).

72

His delicate hand makes a pass through the air and a faintly glowing shield forms before him. You hurl the Shuriken with all your force, hoping to penetrate his aura of enchantment. Make an Attack Roll. If you score 7 or more turn to **49**. If you score less than 7 turn to **60**.

73

You row the boat across the slime-covered swamp, towards the moat, but from the moment that you climbed into it water has been pouring in through the cracks and, as you float out across the moat, the boat begins to sink. To your horror you see that the water is infested with Floating Mouths, voracious fish, all teeth and elastic belly. If you are skilled in Climbing you may try to throw your grappling hook onto the wall of the miniature castle and hope to climb up the rope (turn to **57**). If you are an Acrobat you may wish to attempt an enormous leap to the far side of the moat (turn to **33**). If you do not wish to use these skills, or do not possess them, you dive into the moat and strike out for the castle (turn to **64**).

74

You haul yourself soundlessly from the moat and

begin the difficult climb up the castle wall, using your Cat's Claws to cling onto every available crevice. You are about to peer over the battlements when the slow footsteps of a patrolling guard pass overhead. You cling motionless, flattening yourself against the wall, as, unaccountably, he pauses above you to survey the moat. Your arms are aching with the strain when, after ten minutes, he walks away towards the nearest tower and you cross the battlements. Using the grappling hook and rope you descend quickly to the Castle Bailey below. The hook falls free at a shake of the rope and you catch it. Looking around you realise that you have only penetrated into the outer courtyard, another wall stands between you and the Inner Bailey which surrounds the Great Keep. There is a narrow hole in the wall used for the passing of arms and food when the gate in the wall is shut. If you have the skill of Escapology, you may try to wriggle through it (turn to **277**). Otherwise you may use your Climbing skills to scale the wall of the Inner Bailey (turn to **38**).

75

You climb to the ceiling using your Cat's Claws and noiselessly open a trapdoor that leads to the roof. You climb out under the eaves and onto the slates of the barracks roof before jumping down to the street below. Make a Fate Roll. If Fate smiles on you, turn to **94**. If you are ill-fated, turn to **125**.

76

The priest is not affronted by your refusal to worship his goddess, instead he takes you to his house, near the great domed cathedral and a meal is served to you both. He tells you that the evil men whom you seek are even now nearing the city of

Druath Glennan, on the northern coast of the Sea of the Star. As it is late, you stay in his house for the night. You may restore up to 3 points of Endurance for the rest. When you awaken, you notice that one of your Shuriken lies on a chair beside your bed. There are no scratches or signs of use but a magical rune has been etched upon it, with acid. The priest tells you over breakfast that he has enchanted the throwing star and says that he will pray that Fate will smile upon you. You may add 1 to the dice when using the Enchanted Shuriken. You take your leave of the priest and make for the north gate. Not far from his house you find yourself in a narrow alley when a runaway ox-cart rounds the corner suddenly and bears down on you. Will you leap high into the air and somersault over it so that it passes beneath you (turn to **405**) or dodge to the side – you will be hit, but not crushed under its wheel (turn to **416**)?

77

Make a note of how many times you try to attack the Reaver. Before the morning star connects you drive your fingers at the evil Captain's throat.

BUCCANEER CAPTAIN
Defence against Cobra Strike: 6
Endurance: 12
Damage: 1 Die + 2

If you have defeated the Captain, turn to **58**.

If he is still alive after four attacks, turn to **45**.

Otherwise, he attacks you with his morning star. Your Defence against the ball and chain is 8.

If you are still alive, you may now try the Teeth of the Tiger throw (turn to **87**), the Leaping Tiger kick (turn to **67**) or another straight fingered jab (return to the top of the paragraph).

78

As you run to attack, Runeweaver points his sword at you and mouths a spell. A globe of green energy explodes towards you from the sword tip. If you have Acrobatics you may try to leap into the air, somersault over it and launch yourself at the warrior-magician (turn to **288**). If you are not an Acrobat or do not wish to attempt this, you can try to deflect it with a Shuriken. If you try this, the globe's Defence is 7. If you succeed, turn to **292**. If you miss it, turn to **365**.

79

Your attempt to infiltrate the castle seems to be going well, as, after many adventures, you cross from the wall of the Inner Bailey to the Great Keep. But for all your stealth a keen-eyed guard has glimpsed you in the light of the full moon. Men pour from the Keep towards you and you turn to run, only to find your way blocked by Honoric and the Captain of the Guard. You fell the Captain but the guards are soon upon you and you are unable to block their thrusts and parry the mighty sweep of Honoric's sword at the same time. Your head sails cleanly from your shoulders and Honoric remains undefeated.

80

You step forward to attack but then somersault suddenly, landing at Gorobei's side as his fist flails

61

the air at the spot from which you leapt. He turns but you have surprised him and will find it easier to attack him than if you merely stood before him to trade blows. You may add two to the dice when rolling for your first attack only. Will you:

Feint a punch and then use the Leaping Tiger kick (turn to **17**)?
Pretend to grapple but instead use the Cobra Strike (turn to **35**)?
Raise your foot as if to kick but sidestep and use the Whirlpool Throw (turn to **61**)?

81

As you climb up into Storm Giant's Causeway, the air grows cooler and snow begins to fall. There are no trails, save those of mountain goats and even these are soon covered. You are at the highest point of the pass when a bank of cloud collects above you. Looking up, you see what looks like a titanic statue on the peak of the nearest mountain. The snow falls thickly as a bolt of lightning darts from the peak into the mountainside above. There is a sudden roaring and you begin to run, but the avalanching snow precipitated by the lightning overwhelms you. You are crushed to death.

82

Your fingers jab like rods of steel towards one of your assailants, as you hope to catch him in the armpit where he has no protection from his mail surcoat. You may choose which one to attack.

	1st PRIEST	2nd PRIEST	3rd PRIEST
Defence against Cobra Strike	5	7	6
Endurance	12	14	13
Damage	1 Die +1	1 Die +1	1 Die +1

If you have defeated them, turn to **55**. If any of the priests are still alive, they try to swing their maces into you. If there are 3 still alive, your Defence is 7, if there are 2, your Defence is 8 and if there is only one left, your Defence is 9. You may only block one of their attacks. If you survive their attack, you may try the Forked Lightning Strike (turn to **71**), the Teeth of the Tiger throw (turn to **63**) or jab again (return to the top of the paragraph).

83

The cave is dark and you stare into the blackness until your eyes become accustomed to the gloom, before calling Togawa's name. The skeleton of an elk of the Western Isles, with antlers nearly twenty feet across, lies on the rocky floor. The huge thigh bones have been cracked open for their marrow. You step cautiously forwards, but freeze as you hear what sounds like an ox breathing heavily. You are tensed when a ten-foot tall Rock Hulk attacks. You try to block his heavy blow but it sweeps your arm aside and whirls you against the side of the cave. Lose 4 Endurance. If you are still alive you throw yourself head first to the ground and somersault towards the monster, and then roll upright and lash out with your foot in one fluid movement. The Rock Hulk flails at you, grunting with pain. You dodge its claws but the beast seems impervious to your blows and the battle rages for some time. Suddenly, a

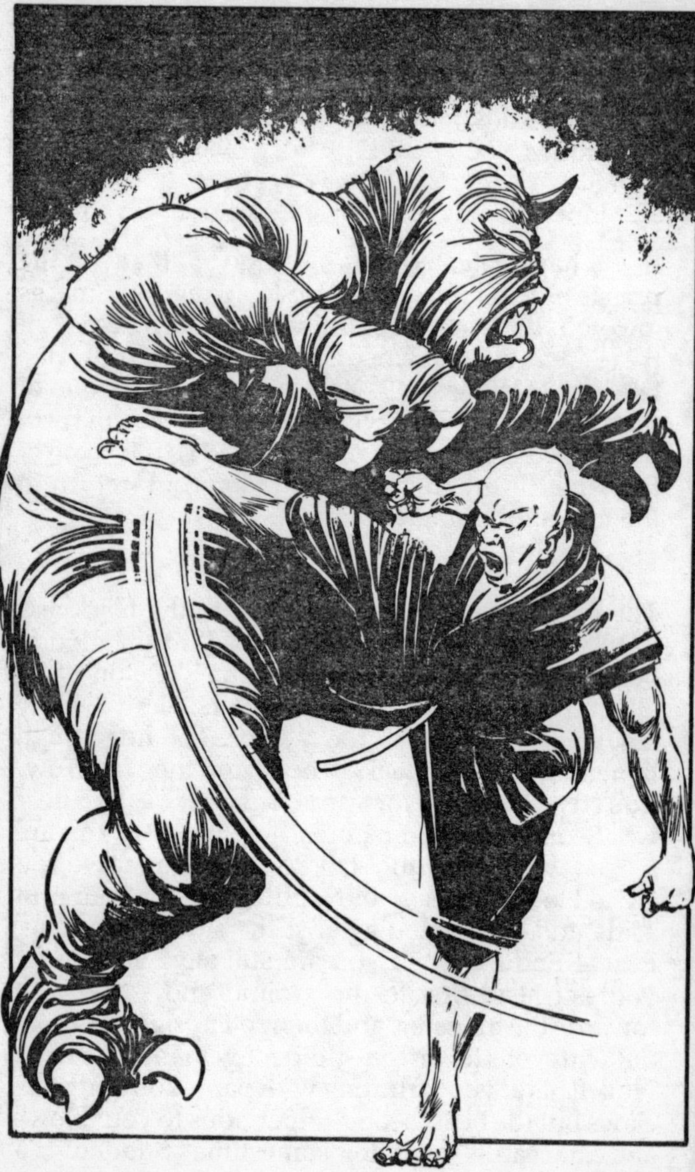

monk appears from nowhere, seemingly in mid-air. The Rock Hulk looks up just as the man lands before it. The monk spins to the right on his left foot, presenting his back to the brute and whips his right foot round and up into the Rock Hulk's midriff with speed even you can hardly believe. He screams as his Inner Force is released and the kick pole-axes the Rock Hulk, which shakes the cave as it falls, rigid, to the floor. The monk turns to you and bows. 'My name is Togawa. Please, follow me.' His own cave is a short climb above that of the Rock Hulk, and you follow him into it. Turn to **66**.

84

You turn sideways and unleash a Winged Horse kick straight at his head, with a cry. Yaemon, anticipating your move, drops onto his back and lashes the ball of his foot into your groin as your kick whips out over his head. You double up in pain as he wraps his feet around your neck and twists savagely, cartwheeling through the air in a variation of the Teeth of the Tiger throw. In agony you cannot control yourself and you fall awkwardly in a heap. Lose 6 Endurance. If you are still alive, you spring to your feet as fast as you can, leaping out of range of Yaemon's attempted chop. However, as you come to a halt, he leaps into the air towards you, his left leg extended, in a flying Winged Horse kick. If you have Acrobatics, turn to **350**. If not, you have no option but to try and block. Your Defence for this is 7. If you succeed, turn to **411**. If you fail, turn to **24**.

85

The bolt of lightning catches you in the side, charring your flesh and jolting you as if you had been hit by a battering ram and you are sent hurtling to the far wall. Lose 8 Endurance. If you are still alive, however, you flip in the air and land safely on your feet, overcoming the pain as the Barbarian moves to attack you with his longsword. You may use the Cobra Strike (turn to 377), the Winged Horse kick (turn to 302), the Dragon's Tail throw (turn to 318) or, if you are skilled with Poison Needles, you may wish to use one (turn to 8).

86

You slink soundlessly as a black panther towards the unsuspecting guard who is leaning against the doorpost lost in thought. Will you creep along the wall and garotte him (turn to 116) or send a Shuriken spinning towards his throat (turn to 105)?

87

Make a note of how many times you try to hit the Reaver. Ducking beneath the flailing chain and ball you jump into the air, and try to clamp your feet around his neck and, by twisting vigorously, throw him into the sea.

BUCCANEER CAPTAIN
Defence against throw: 6
Endurance: 12
Damage: 1 Die

If this is your fourth attack and the Reaver is still alive turn to 45.

If you have successfully thrown him, he is whipped over the edge of the stern castle and into the sea. Turn to 34.

If you have failed to throw him he attacks you with his morning star and your Defence is 7.

If you are still alive, you may now use the Cobra Strike (turn to 77) or use the Leaping Tiger (turn to 67).

88

Only Yaemon notices you slipping the needle into your mouth and when you turn and spit the needle at him he snaps his fingers up and deftly catches it between finger and thumb, inches before his face. 'Kill him,' he says, and Manse the Deathmage, eager to show off his skill, obliges. He holds his hand out towards you as if he were cupping an orange and beckons slightly. To your horror your heart bursts out from your chest and flies into his hand. He squeezes the still pulsing organ and the floor is drenched with your blood as you fall dead.

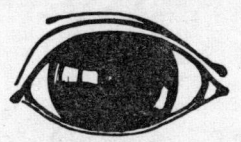

89

You cartwheel toward Yaemon and launch into the attack. Will you punch (turn to 266), kick (turn to 390) or throw (turn to 401)?

90

His delicate hands make a pass through the air and a faintly glowing shield forms before him, blocking the needle. He begins another spell, his glowing eyes smouldering with hatred and you decide to attack him hand to hand. Turn to 413.

91

The rain abates slightly as you strike your way slowly across the moat. You hear the grating of a guard's heel on gravel as he turns to look out over the water, worried by the sudden silence of the bullfrogs. You slip below the surface. Make a Fate Roll. If Fate smiles on you, the guard turns away, turn to **74**. If Fate turns her back on you, turn to **108**.

92

Olvar lets out a ferocious cry as, throwing caution to the wind, he whirls his sword above his head and then lunges at you. He is berserk, lost in a battle frenzy. He will feel no fear or pain until either you or he lie dead. Subtract one from any damage you do to him. You parry his blade with your forearm, side-step and unleash a Cobra Strike from your hip.

OLVAR THE BARBARIAN
Defence against Cobra Strike: 6
Endurance: 18
Damage: 1 Die + 2

If you have defeated Olvar, turn to **47**. If he still lives, he swings his sword in a great arc from left to right, trying to cut open your chest. Your Defence against his savage cut is 8 as you try to leap backwards.

If you still live, you may kick (turn to **23**), throw (turn to **39**) or punch again (return to the top of this paragraph).

93

The wild lands give way to the meadows of the valley of the River Fortune. You pass the tracks of strange beasts everywhere and, skirting a dense and gloomy wood, you find a wide swathe trampled in the meadow grass. Bending down to examine the tracks you see that they were made by a large band of Orcs, returning, perhaps to the Rift, a few days ago. As you sniff the air, a man staggers towards you, out of the waist high grass. He is old and wears a blue robe that is in tatters but it is his face that holds your attention. It is encrusted with blood for his eyes have been gouged out. You call to him and he sits down suddenly, saying that he has no gold and that he has a terrible disease that you would catch if you ate him. You reassure him that you are not a cannibal and ask him what happened. He tells you that he is a monk from Fiendil. He is losing track of time but he thinks that he has felt the sun on his face four times since a man called Honoric had him blinded for spying through a keyhole. 'He was with a Grandmaster of our order, a fine man named Yaemon and I saw them planning a journey north on a map, but Yaemon heard me and I was caught. Help me, I'm starving, which way is the river?' You tell him to walk downhill if he wishes to find the river, and taking pity on him, give him some nuts which you have gathered. He remembers only that they were planning to meet a third man whom they called the Deathmage. There is nothing further you can do to help him and so you journey on towards the city of Fiendil. Turn to **260**.

94

You drop head-first towards the ground twenty feet below, and turning in mid-air, land on your feet like a cat. No one has noticed you and you glide through the night to the city gate like a shadow. At the gate you distract the attention of the guards by throwing a stone which shatters a pane of glass, near a thief who thought he was unobserved, and slip out of the city at the first ray of dawn, as the guards run to arrest him. Turn to **65**.

95

Gorobei has used the Iron Fist, punching you so hard in the back of the neck that you slump to the granite floor, senseless. A young village boy is pouring water onto your forehead when you regain your wits. A few of the younger acolytes murmur condolences as you rub your neck. An hour later Gorobei returns from the robing chamber and you applaud with the others as he is ordained as a Grandmaster. Turn to **191**.

96

You are among them before they can finish whatever fell incantation they had begun and they heft their maces at you instead. They are in full chainmail, well protected but slow. Will you use the Teeth of the Tiger throw (turn to **63**), the Cobra Strike jab (turn to **82**) or the Forked Lightning kick (turn to **71**)?

97

One of the buccaneers has seen you and he creeps along the deck of the Watery Grave intent on severing your hands from your wrists with his cutlass. The faintest jingling of his many ear-rings alerts you and you nimbly vault over the rail onto the deck, and catch his arm with your left hand as he swings his cutlass at your head. Then you use the Whirlpool to throw him over the side. Turning, you run up the stairway to the stern castle from where the pirate Captain is directing his men. You bound up the last steps to appear from nowhere before him. He steps back in surprise but soon regains his composure. He is a large man, with a grizzled beard and gold armbands which cause the veins of his massive arms to stand out like cords. He swings his morning star at you as you move in to attack. Which move will you use: The Leaping Tiger (turn to **67**)? The Cobra Strike (turn to **77**)? The Teeth of the Tiger (turn to **87**)?

98

As you wade through the swamp the Shaggoth turns with a horrible slurping sound and the Dark Elf fights her way free of the suckered tentacles. She smiles her gratitude, her eyes, like huge almonds, narrowing. You turn to face the Shaggoth together but you are suddenly pitched forwards into the folds of its putrescent flesh by a blow from the Elf's sword. Laughing cruelly, she wades to the boat as you vainly try to free yourself from the slime beast's grip. It sinks slowly into the swamp, pulling you with it, and your nose and lungs fill with filth as you struggle helplessly. When the swamp dries out not even your bones will remain.

99

You are watched constantly but find time to examine the lock of the gateway that leads to the Inner Bailey and to find a hole in the wall, used for passing food and arms through when the gate is shut. When it is time, you are taken into the Keep itself. The main hall has a large spiral staircase which leads to the castle roof and thence to the three turrets.

You are ushered into the parlour before dinner to entertain Yaemon and Honoric; Manse the Deathmage is nowhere to be seen. Yaemon watches you intently but Honoric is at ease, pouring wine from a flagon into a golden goblet. The Captain of the castle and his lady sit between them. You sing a Manmarcher song of brave deeds in battle and lost loves and your juggling raises polite applause. As soon as your act is finished the Captain signals and your escort, two guards, usher you out of the parlour, just as Manse enters from the door opposite. If you have the skill of Poison Needles, you may wish to use it against Yaemon (turn to **88**). If you do not or prefer not to, you allow the guards to escort you out of the castle (turn to **418**).

100

As you kneel before the great altar in the vast vaults of the domed cathedral, Fate accepts you as her reverencer. At the same time, your own god, Kwon, renounces you, and your Inner Force is stripped away, leaving you weakened. This does not worry you, for now you know that it was fated that this should come to pass and that it would be pointless to regret. Your quest to kill Yaemon seems unimportant and you idle your days in the dreamy city of Fiendil as a priest in the cathedral, until one day even the calm folk of the city seem agitated. A great darkness, a long night without days, is followed by news that the dread Legion of the Sword of Doom and the monks of the Scarlet Mantis have sacked the Spires of Foreshadowing and now march on Fiendil. It is too late. Kwon is incarcerated in Inferno but your failure does not trouble you.

101

As you pass through the archway at the bottom of the steps you see Yaemon on the roof of the Great

Keep. He bears the Mantis tattoo on his forehead and wears the scarlet jacket and loose trousers of the Order of the Scarlet Mantis. He is in his middle years but his body is supple and powerful. The corded muscles on his forearms ripple as he clenches his fists. He bows to you and then says, 'You have been at your work, Ninja.'

You return his bow saying, 'My tasks are not yet done.'

He smiles and replies, 'I killed your spiritual father, as I had killed your real father when you were but a babe-in-arms. Now, I shall kill you.' No-one has ever spoken to you of the death of your father but Yaemon's words only cause the desire for revenge to flare stronger within you. You master your anger and calm yourself, ready to give battle. Yaemon has been Grandmaster of the Flame for longer than your lifetime. You could not fear to meet a more experienced adept at the deadly Way of the Mantis. His body is at a peak of perfection and his will is strong. You move towards him realising that this will be a battle like no other. Yaemon's Endurance is 20. Will you:

Run to attack? Turn to **89**.
Close and use Poison Needles if you have that skill? Turn to **69**.
Unleash a stream of 3 Shuriken, if you have that many? Turn to **51**.

102

The Amulet shatters, the shards twinkling as they tumble down the staircase like the pieces of a smashed vase. The Deathmage is surprised that you have withstood his infernal sorcery, but he begins another spell. His arcane words conjure visions of primordial evils and the malevolence of long forgotten gods. If you have skill with Poison Needles you may wish to use one (turn to **90**). Otherwise, will you leap to the attack (turn to **413**) or hurl a Shuriken (turn to **72**)?

103
You turn and run but as they finish their fell incantation your movements slow, your limbs feel as heavy as lead and it is only by a great effort of will that, quivering with the strain, you can get them to move at all. You stagger to the river and duck out of sight in some bullrushes. Will you slide into the river and stay below the surface, using your slender bamboo tube to breath through (turn to **4**) or roll a boulder into the river and crawl slowly away through the bullrushes (turn to **123**)?

104
'Ah, yes,' says the guard, 'it is a fair city. I sailed there once in a ship. In you go then . . .' You thank him and walk under the portcullis into the bailey beyond. Turn to **112**.

105
The Shuriken finds its mark. The guard throws his hand to his throat and screams before collapsing to the floor, dead. Realising the alarm may have been given, you run out of the barracks towards the city gate, leaving your throwing star behind (cross it off your Character Sheet). Turn to **125**.

106
The Barbarian tenses as you place the needle on your rolled tongue and spit it out in one fluid

motion. The needle imbeds itself in his cheek. He has an iron constitution and although a look of agony twists his features, his system overcomes the virulent poison. You may note that he has lost 4 Endurance. As you pause in astonishment, he strikes at you, and his sword cleaves the air towards your shoulder. Your Defence against his blow is 8 as you try to bring your left forearm up to sweep aside the blade. If he hits you, his sword will do 1 Die + 1 damage. If you survive you may use the Cobra Strike (turn to **92**), the Winged Horse (turn to **23**) or the Dragon's Tail (turn to **39**).

107

You swing up over the rail, unseen, and run up the stairway to the stern castle from where the pirate Captain is directing his men. You bound up the last steps, to appear from nowhere before him. He steps back in surprise but soon regains his composure. He is a large man, with a grizzled beard and gold armbands, which cause the veins of his massive arms to stand out like cords. He swings his morning star at you as you move in to attack. Which move will you use:

The Leaping Tiger (turn to **67**)?
The Cobra Strike (turn to **77**)?
The Teeth of the Tiger (turn to **87**)?

108

You use your breathing tube for air, but after ten minutes in the freezing moat, decide to risk crawling out to begin your climb. The grappling hook, its prongs muted with felt, lodges fast, and you move up to the battlements swiftly and soundlessly. As you peep your head above the battlements a strange terror grips you and for an instant you are frozen in fear. It is long enough for Honoric to bury his Eldritch Sword, Sorcerak, in your head, and you tumble backwards into the moat, dead. One of the guards had heard you in the moat when the frogs stopped their croaking.

109

You clasp your hands around its forearm – it is too cumbersome to dodge but instead flame bursts forth all over its body and you are badly burnt. Lose 4 Endurance. If you are still alive, as you spring back unable to attempt the Whirlpool, its fiery fist descends on you. Your Defence as you try to somersault aside, is 6.

EFREET
Damage: 2 Dice + 1

If you are still alive, you may use the Iron Fist punch (turn to 131) or the Leaping Tiger kick (turn to 119).

110

Your last blow sent Gorobei tumbling senseless to the granite floor. A ripple of applause greets your victory and the Grandmaster of the Dawn compliments you on your fighting prowess and beckons you into the robing chamber. You step beyond the Temple Hall through silken drapes into a small dark room, completely bare of furnishing save for two enormous copper chests. Incense is burning in a censer which swings from the ceiling like a pendulum. The room is lit by white candles. You kneel on the rush matting facing the three Grandmasters who stare ahead, unseeing, waiting for you to break the silence which you are determined to keep. After an hour-candle has sputtered its last, during which time none of you has moved so much as a muscle the Grandmaster of the Dawn looks into your eyes and says, 'Kwon knows that you desire in your heart to serve him but I must ask you two questions. Do you truly desire to serve Kwon above all other things or do you desire to avenge the death of your foster-father, Naijishi, more even than to serve your God? What should a Ninja fear most – the failure of a mission or capture by an enemy who will use torture to gain secrets?' You know that in your heart of hearts you would rather avenge Naijishi than anything else in Orb but a Grandmaster should dedicate his life to Kwon. As for the second question, you can only let your good sense guide you. Do you answer:

'I desire to serve Kwon above all else and I fear only failure of a mission' (turn to **139**)?
'I desire to avenge the father who loved me and I fear torture above all' (turn to **151**)?
'I desire to avenge the father who loved me and I fear only failure of a mission' (turn to **177**)?
'I desire to serve Kwon above all else and I fear torture above all' (turn to **128**)?

111

The Snow Giant falls onto the ice with a crack, unmoving. Its blood stains the frosty surface a rosy pink. Panting for breath, you look around and see that the knight lies dead, poisoned by the Cobra Man who is chasing the man in blue and gold robes. You move to the moat side of the ice and manage to break a small ice-floe away from its edge. You give it a great heave towards the castle and jump on to it. Looking into the moat you can see it is infested with Floating Mouths, voracious fish that are all teeth and elastic belly. As you float gently across, the man in blue and gold robes grabs a long pole and, using magic, rises gently into the air, to the applause of the crowd. He pushes himself towards the castle with the pole, and you arrive at the other side of the moat together. Turn to 372.

112

You saunter across the courtyard towards the Bailiff's office. The two men in black travelling robes, Honoric and Manse the Deathmage, are talking to the Captain of the Guard and a group of his men. You stop to watch at a distance as Honoric, a powerfully built man with an arrogant and cruel look about him, borrows the Captain's weapon and invites the soldiers to attack him. Several do so at once but there is no way past his flashing sword. He disarms three of them, then beats the rest back – all they can do is fend off his blows and you know that he could kill them at will. Seeing this display, Manse grimaces sourly and, pointing, turns the sword which Honoric is holding into a tulip. The Captain of the Guard cannot resist chuckling at the sight of this huge man the Marshal of the Legion of the Sword of Doom, clutching a tulip with which to belabour the soldiers. Honoric turns red with rage and, flinging the flower down, he draws his own great black sword. A chill of horror grips you and the guards cower as a pall of fear descends upon the castle. The wicked blade smokes slightly and the tulip has turned back into a sword.

'Where is your magic now, Deathmage, your spells

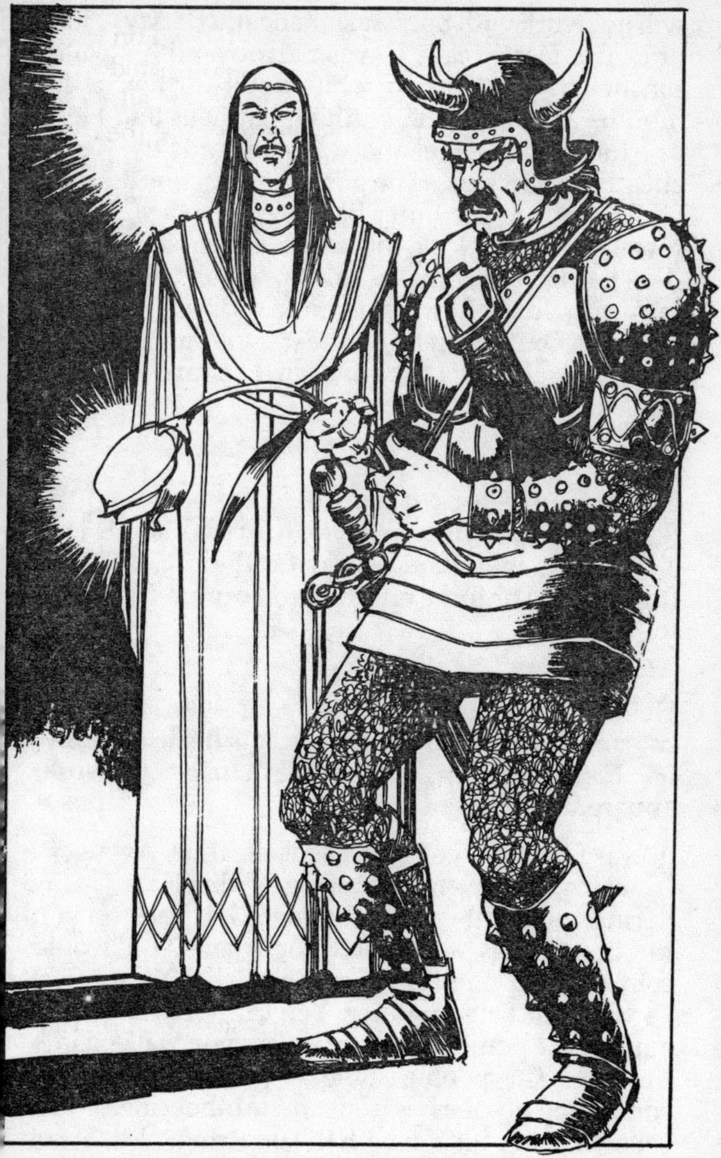

will not work with Sorcerak unsheathed,' says Honoric. The Deathmage's eyes narrow and his pallid pinched face seems to whiten still further as he mouths another spell. Nothing happens and Honoric turns on his heel and walks towards the Keep, sheathing Sorcerak as he goes. As he opens the gate which leads to the Inner Bailey you catch sight of a tower at the back of the castle which seems part derelict. It would make an easy climb. The Bailiff tells you that they have hired 'a real Bard' for tomorrow but when he has heard you sing and seen you juggle, he says that you can do a turn at dinner that evening. Turn to **99**.

113

You scramble back down the scree slopes to the floor of Fortune Pass. Will you turn back south and, skirting the mountains, make for the city of Fiendil (turn to **122**) or forge on through Fortune Pass (turn to **70**)?

114

He sees the deadly intent in your eyes an instant before your blow lands, but accepts death stoically. His neck is broken, but he still manages to speak, apparently resigned to it all.

'It was fated that you should kill me thus, Avenger.' It seems, however, that Fate is displeased. The hermit revered her and she turns her back on you for the callous act which she knew you would commit. You almost feel your luck change, subtract 2 from your Fate Modifier. You cannot help quietly cursing the pointlessness of it all as you walk on into the city. The people smile at you as you go by, something no-one has done in the other cities. They seem to float past you with the uncaring calmness of those who accept that their destiny has already been decided. Turn to **185**.

115

After nightfall you strain at your bonds but the only reward for your efforts is the kiss of the whip. Exhausted, you fall asleep before dawn and awake to find iron manacles around your wrists and a girdle around your middle by which you are chained to the oar. They are heavy and unbreakable and will not be struck off until your body is spent and lifeless after years at the oar. You have failed.

116

Silently, you pause behind the guard, readying yourself to strike. With blinding speed, you wrap the garotte around his throat. The guard dies without a sound as the wire slices neatly through his windpipe and you slip out of the barracks and glide through the night to the city gate like a shadow. At the gate, you distract the attention of the gate guards by throwing a stone that shatters a pane of glass near a thief, who thought he was unobserved, and slip out of the city at the first ray of dawn, as the guards run to arrest him. Turn to **65**.

117

As the dust enters the flames there is a brilliant flash. You had shaded your eyes, but Olvar is, for the moment, blinded. The Barbarian backs out of the doorway and you follow up with a flying Winged Horse to his chest and he throws his arms up and crashes backwards into the snow. Note that he has lost 5 Endurance, for you have cracked some of his ribs. You are about to run out into the snow to finish him, when a bolt of blue lightning discharges from the gem at his forehead towards the doorway. You flip backwards into the air, somersault as the bolt passes beneath you, and land upright facing the doorway. Olvar has regained his sight and he charges in. Will you use the Winged Horse kick (turn to **302**), the Cobra Strike (turn to **377**), the Dragon's Tail throw (turn to **318**)? Of if you have the skill of Poison Needles and wish to use one, turn to **8**.

118

He chops his right hand at the left side of your neck. You bring your leg up in an arc from left to right, sweeping his arm aside, but he pulls it back and chops again at the other side of your neck. Giving ground fast, you twist your arm up across your chest to take the blow on your forearm. With unrelenting rapidity, Yaemon closes his hand into a fist and snaps his arm straight, trying to drive his knuckles into the bridge of your nose. You are hard pressed, but you manage to bring your forearm back and across the top of your head, just in time to intercept the blow. Barely moments later, he whiplashes the side of his right foot at your throat in a Winged Horse kick but, with a speed born of desperation, you manage to slap his foot aside with your left hand. The force of the kick spins him around, and you take the chance to leap back out of range, whilst the sound of his shouts echo into the night. Yaemon is turning to face you and you seize the opportunity to counter attack. Will you kick (turn to **301**), punch (turn to **266**), or throw (turn to **401**)?

119

Flame ripples across its massive frame as the Elemental Being tries to grab you. You kick with all your might hoping to make some impression on the fiery colossus. If you manage to hit it, you must subtract one from your Endurance as the flames sear your foot.

EFREET
Defence against Leaping Tiger: 5
Endurance: 22
Damage: 2 Dice + 1

If you win, turn to **197**. If the Efreet still stands before you, it tries to knock you to the ground with both its huge fists. Your Defence against these hammer blows is 7.

If you survive you may use the Iron Fist (turn to **131**), the Whirlpool throw (turn to **109**) or kick again (return to the top of this paragraph).

120

You raise yourself soundlessly from the moat and make the easy climb to the top of the crumbling tower, lashed by wind and rain. As you peer over the battlements you can see two guards standing by a fire which has been lit under a large tarred sheet of canvas. The fire is some way from the top of the staircase leading to the Inner Bailey which surrounds the Great Keep. You duck below the battlement again and hang, as the clouds break allowing the moon to shine through. Five minutes later the moon is again hidden and you creep soundlessly over the battlements onto the tower roof. Will you hurl a Shuriken at one of the guards and run forwards to garotte the second (turn to **11**), throw a small rock into the fire (turn to **355**) or if you have some flash powder throw this into the fire (turn to **415**)?

121

You grab the small boat as the Shaggoth sinks slowly into the mire, dragging the struggling Dark Elf with it. She gives vent to a bubbling scream as she sinks slowly beneath the surface. To your dismay the boat is full of cracks and holes and has let in a great deal of swampy water. Will you jump in and try to row it to the moat (turn to **73**) or abandon it and drag yourself over to the desert dunes (turn to **134**)?

122

The going is difficult as you skirt the rough foothills of the Mountains of Vision and the journey takes many days longer than you had anticipated. After the hardest day's slog you have yet driven yourself through, night falls. The moon is red and no day follows. You are too late. The eternal darkness has come and Kwon has been imprisoned in Inferno. Your Inner Force drains away and there is nothing you can do to stop the rise of evil. You have failed.

123

The priests rush to the river's edge and stare into the water at the point where the boulder splashed. The sluggishness wears off and you glide through the bullrushes and away, as they peer in. One is casting away his chainmail ready to explore the depths of the river as you vanish into the hills that ring the city of Mortavalon. You rejoin the road and, rounding a corner espy a cave overhung with rock in the hillside above you. Will you continue straight on to Mortavalon (turn to **283**) or enter the cave (turn to **275**)?

124

'Ah ha, I was in Druath as well, a shame I missed you, where did you sing?' Will you reply:

The Allmother hostel (turn to **48**)?
The Hydra's Heads (turn to **22**)?
In the Main Square (turn to **62**)?

125

You glide through the night towards the city gate but someone has spotted you. The alarm sounds at the barracks as you approach the gate, and torches flare on the gate tower, some of which are thrown down into the street nearby. You hear the unmistakable twang of crossbow springs and spin towards the sound. Do you have the skill of Arrow Cutting? If you do, turn to **201**. If you do not, turn to **136**.

126

Using your Escapologist's skill you had tensed your body and held your limbs so that, though the buccaneers bound you tightly, when you relaxed the ropes were loosened. You wriggle and twist, using the amazing suppleness of your body to loosen the bonds further. Dislocating a shoulder, you succeed in freeing an arm and then quickly dispose of the ropes which confine you. In the darkness of the oar deck you are thankful for the diet which has given you unusual powers of seeing in the dark. The duty guard doesn't hear you as you steal past the sleeping bodies at the oars, until you are close enough to wrap a handy piece of chain around his neck and choke him into unconsciousness. He crumples without a sound and you step over his body to the locker where they have stowed your Ninja tools and retrieve them. One by one you free the crew and tell them to wait quietly for your signal, whilst you go to the main cabin, to see if the buccaneer Captain is sleeping aboard his prize. Silently, you climb the stairs to the main deck and wait for the moon to pass behind a cloud. You reach the door of the main cabin unnoticed. Can you Pick Locks? If you can and you wish to do so turn to **153**. If you cannot or do not wish to, you can use Inner Force to punch and smash the door open (turn to **137**).

127

The lightning bolt lances past you and sets the planks of the hut smouldering. Runeweaver was closer to the fire-flash than Olvar and his sight will not return for some time. You spring to attack the Barbarian who is ready for you with his sword, shaking his head to clear his vision. You may use the Cobra Strike jab at his unprotected neck (turn to **92**), the Winged Horse kick (turn to **23**), the Dragon's Tail throw (turn to **39**) or, if you have the Poison Needle skill, you may wish to use one (turn to **106**).

128

The Grandmaster shakes his head. 'You have answered neither truthfully nor wisely. You cannot hide your wish to avenge Naijishi who loved you and taught you to love our Lord Kwon, from we who have known you near all of your short life. It is not wrong that you should wish to avenge Naijishi but you must wait patiently for your time to come and never forget that the service of Kwon is the helping of all mankind. As for torture, it is only through failing a mission that a true Ninja could be captured and there is always time to bite one's tongue from one's head and bleed to death rather than risk betraying secrets. You need fear only the failure of a mission. You have failed the spiritual test and you are not yet worthy to become Grandmaster of the Five Winds. Go back to the Temple Hall and ask Gorobei to come in to us.'

Dejectedly, you return to the main temple and there is a low moan from the villagers as you ask Gorobei to go into the robing room. He places his arm on your shoulder and says, 'Next time,' before moving past the silken curtain. An hour later he returns and you applaud with the others as he is ordained as a Grandmaster. Turn to **191**.

129

The horse, too, is affected and it slows to a plodding walk, whinnying shrilly in terror. Your body quivers as you strive to move but you cannot. The priests, for you know this is priestly magic, knock you from the saddle and tie you securely. If you have a Ring, they take it from you – cross it off your Character Sheet. Are you a skilled Escapologist? If you are, turn to **21**. If you are not, turn to **37**.

130

You pass through the archway which leads to the tower topped by the banner of the Black Whirlpool. The spiral staircase is lit by an ominous green luminescence and you see a red eye, hanging disembodied in space at the top of the stone steps. It

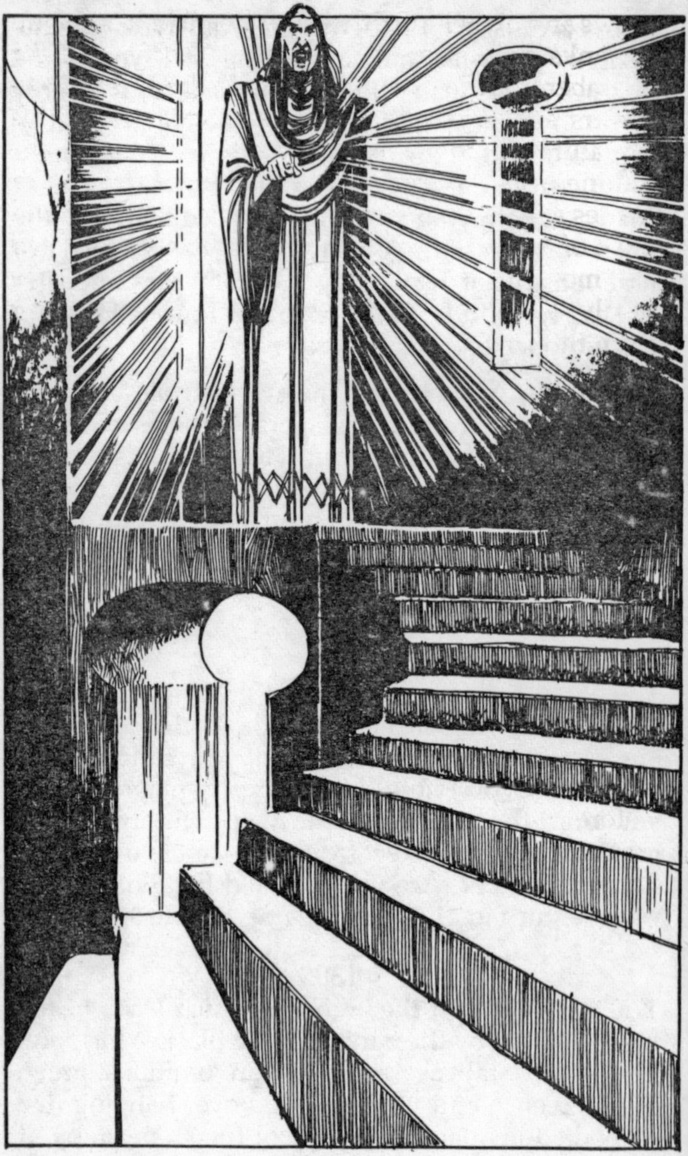

glows and the white of the eye is horribly bloodshot. It blinks once, then disappears as the door to the chamber above flies open. Manse the Deathmage towers above you at the top of the staircase, his unnatural white pallor turned ghastly green in the luminescence. His eyes glow bloodshot-red and he carries a blackwood staff topped with the head and neck of a hooded cobra of carven jade. Before you can move he points a long finger at you and says coldly, 'DIE!' Do you have the Amulet of Protection from the Finger of Death? If you do, turn to **102**. If you do not, turn to **140**.

131

The fiery elemental being is cumbersome and you can scarcely miss, your only worry is that it may not feel pain from your blow. If you hit it, subtract one from your Endurance as your fist is burned by the flames which lick across its body.

EFREET
Defence against Iron Fist: 4
Endurance: 22
Damage: 2 Die + 1

If you win, turn to **197**. If the Efreet still stands before you, it tries to drive its flaming fist down into your chest. Your Defence against this blow as you try to cartwheel aside, is 7.

If you survive, you may use the Leaping Tiger kick (turn to **119**), the Whirlpool throw (turn to **109**) or punch again (return to the top of this paragraph).

132

The rain abates slightly as you stroke your way slowly across the moat. You hear the grating of a guard's heel on gravel as he turns to look out over the water, worried by the sudden silence of the bullfrogs. You slip below the surface. Make a Fate Roll. If Fate smiles on you, turn to **120**. If Fate turns her back on you, turn to **108**.

133

The rock-face towers above you and you realise that it will be a dangerous climb. If you wish to go on you will be in the hands of Fate (turn to **173**). If you would rather not take this risk and abandon the chance to find Togawa, if he still lives, turn to **113**.

134

As you near the sunken platform that separates the swamp from the desert, near the arena wall, there is a bubbling in the mire ahead of you. You change direction and, planting your foot on a mossy hummock, launch yourself into the air and flip over the high fence of iron spikes, drawing another gasp from the crowd. You land on your feet and survey the arena for a moment. The Dark Elf and the Shaggoth are nowhere to be seen. The man in blue and gold robes has slain the Snow Giant but the knight in armour lies in an awkward position on the dunes, with the Cobra Man towering over him. A long thin pole is propped up in a dune near the knight's body. You decide to attack the Cobra Man to gain the pole, hoping to vault across the moat. The Cobra Man's head sways hypnotically above yours; he is waiting to strike. Will you use the Tiger Paw chop (turn to **42**), the Winged Horse kick (turn to **25**) or the Teeth of the Tiger throw (turn to **13**)?

135

The priests dismount and, walking slowly towards you, begin a fell incantation. Your limbs begin to feel heavy. Will you run to attack them (turn to **44**), run to the river and, hiding in the bullrushes roll a boulder in before crawling away (turn to **123**) or run to the river and, diving in, stay submerged using your bamboo tube (turn to **4**)?

136
You try to roll aside but a crossbow bolt slams into your side and you sprawl flat on the ground. Lose 4 Endurance. The gate guards charge towards you, as you spring to your feet. Are you an Acrobat? If you are, turn to **144**. If not, turn to **285**.

137
You stand, legs apart, in front of the door, taking three slow deep breaths. Then, when you are ready, you use the Iron Fist with a grunting cry as the Inner Force escapes you. There is a crash and the door flies off its hinges. You leap over it as it falls to the floor. Cross one point of Inner Force from your Character Sheet. The buccaneer Captain is inside having forsaken his ship for the comfort of the Aquamarin. Woken from his sleep by the crash of the door he rolls off the bed, pulling his cutlass from under the pillow, and tries to throw some blankets at you. You whip out a Shuriken and with a deft flick of the

wrist, send it hurtling towards him, before he can cry out. Make a Shuriken Roll. The Captain's Defence against the Shuriken is 5. If you succeed, turn to **164**. If you fail, turn to **175**.

138

As you steal towards the castle moat in the moonlight, on this still night, your acute sense of hearing picks up a stifled shout from the castle battlement. You have been spotted. You lie low for a time but as soon as you hear the yapping of hounds, decide to run away to the woods. You use your knowledge of woodcraft to throw the dogs off the scent and return to the castle the following day. Turn to **166**.

139

The Grandmaster smiles and shakes his head. 'You have answered cleverly but not truthfully. You cannot hide your wish to avenge Naijishi, who loved you and taught you to love our Lord Kwon, from we who have known you near all of your short life. It is not wrong that you should wish for revenge on Yaemon but wait patiently for your time to come and never forget that the service of Kwon is the helping of all mankind. You are right, though, to say that a Ninja need only fear failure, for to endure torture one must first endure failure. There is always time to bite one's tongue from one's head and bleed to death rather than risk betraying secrets under torture. I shall not say that you have failed, rather you are like a whetted blade straining in the sheath needing only the wisdom of years to hone you to perfection. I shall not keep such a potent weapon sheathed – you have passed the test.'

They lead you back to the Temple Hall where the

monks and villagers have waited to see whether you would pass the test. Prayers to Kwon are offered up as part of the ceremony at which you are ordained as Grandmaster of the Five Winds. Gorobei applauds with the others. For now he remains an Adept of the Inner Circle but his time will come for he is a great warrior and a good monk. Should you die he will probably take your place. Turn to **191**.

140

Your heart palpitates wildly, then explodes from your chest and flies into the Deathmage's outstretched hand. He squeezes the still pulsing organ and the steps above you are drenched with your blood. You fall back dead and roll head over heels to the roof of the Great Keep below. Without protection from the infernal sorcery of Manse you could not stand against him.

141

You cross the roof of the Great Keep and enter the turret which flies the flag of the Black Whirlpool. With Sorcerak at your back you climb to the top of the turret. The staircase is lit by an ominous green luminescence and you see a red eye, hanging disembodied in space at the top of the stone steps. It glows and the white of the eye is horribly bloodshot. It seems to pop suddenly and disappears as you climb the last steps and throw open the door at their top. Manse the Deathmage still clad in his black cloak which accentuates the pallor of his features, rises from the bed as you enter. The fear which emanates from the Eldritch blade of Sorcerak sets his white hair on end. He mouths a spell, but nothing happens. You throw Sorcerak to the floor before him and he shrinks back. His eyes glow red like the one which you saw outside his chamber.

His voice is a low hiss as he threatens 'Kill me and that fell sword will take your soul.' You ignore him and he tries one last spell as you advance, but Sorcerak dispels the magic as a bolt of fire leaves his mouth and you throw him easily to the floor. He is not strong and struggles ineffectually as you grind your heel into his neck. It snaps like a twig. Never again will Manse the Deathmage offer up children for sacrifice to his god Nemesis. With Honoric's sword you have rid Orb of its most powerful black magician. Leaving Sorcerak to smoke on the floor of the chamber you descend the staircase of the turret intent on finding Yaemon and avenging your spiritual father. Turn to **305**.

142

The bolt of lightning catches you in the side, charring your flesh and jolting you as if you had been hit by a battering ram and you are sent hurtling to the far wall. Lose 8 Endurance. However, if you are still alive, you flip in the air and land safely on your feet. You manage to overcome the pain as the Barbarian moves to attack you with his longsword. Runeweaver was closer to the fire-flash than Olvar and his sight will not return for some time. You may use the Cobra Strike (turn to **92**), the Winged Horse kick (turn to **23**), the Dragon's Tail throw (turn to **39**) or, if you are skilled with Poison Needles, you may wish to use one (turn to **106**).

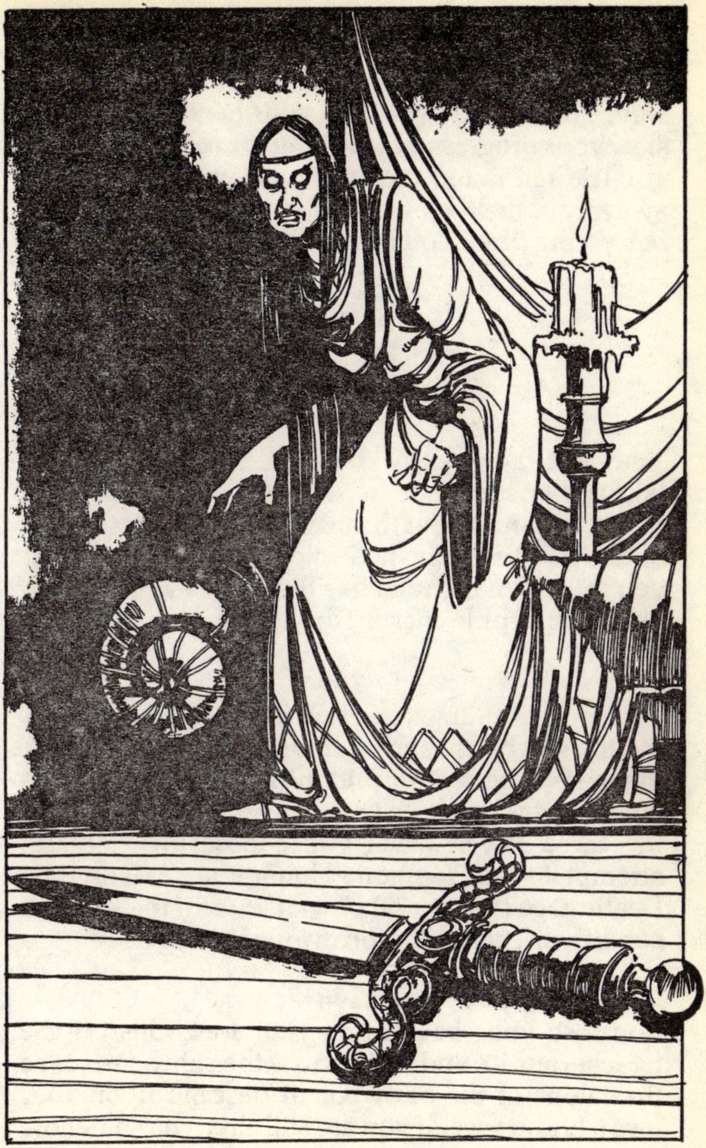

143

As you are nearing a cave mouth in the sheer rock, a small ledge of rock on which you are standing gives way. You fall, trying to use your hands and feet to slow your progress by brushing the rock-face as you go. The fall is too far, however, and you bounce away from the rock-face and are impaled on the tip of a young pine. You have failed the quest.

144

You wait, apparently dejected, for the guards to take you prisoner but then somersault high in the air over them and sprint through the gate at the first ray of dawn. The astonished soldiers run after you but you sail down the road like the wind and they soon give up the futile chase. Turn to **254**.

145

You conceal yourself in a hole in the ground, watching the gatehouse and wait for darkness to fall. The moon is white and full and the night is still. There is not even enough breeze to spread the banners atop the three towers. Will you choose this night to attempt to kill Yaemon, Honoric and Manse the Deathmage (turn to **79**) or wait to see if the weather conditions change tomorrow night (turn to **7**)?

146

You lose your balance as your foot slips on the treacherous ice and slide across the shiny surface as the talons of the Snow Giant descend upon you, lose 6 Endurance. If you are still alive you somehow manage to regain your feet as the crowd howl with blood-lust, and attack again using the Iron Fist punch, striking upwards from your crouched position at the white hulk.

SNOW GIANT
Defence against Punch: 5
Endurance: 22
Damage: 1 Die + 3

If you have killed the Snow Giant turn to **111**. If the Snow Giant is still alive its talons rake at your face. Your Defence against this great sweep of its arm as you fight for your balance on the ice is 6. If you are still alive you may use the Forked Lightning Strike kick (turn to **184**), slide beneath its flailing arms and use the Dragon's Tail throw (turn to **202**) or punch again (turn to **160**).

147

You empty the Essence of Firenewt powder on the surface of the moat and it stimulates the bullfrogs to recommence their croaking. Turn to **120**.

148

You walk silently to the archway at the bottom of the turret, above which flies the Scarlet Mantis banner and stepping carefully you glide up the stone steps, feeling for traps as you go. Turn to **361**.

149

The Efreet towers above you, flame licking across its ruby flesh. It reaches for you, and fire pours down its arm. Will you use the Iron Fist punch (turn to **131**), the Whirlpool throw (turn to **109**) or the Leaping Tiger kick (turn to **119**)?

150

You are looking sideways at Yaemon. You hop, crab-like into range and unleash another Forked Lightning Strike kick, driving your foot at his groin. Yaemon is not so easily fooled a second time and he leaps high over your first strike and, still in the air, kicks you in the face before you can finish your Forked Lightning Strike. You stagger back and he lands in front of you. Placing his left hand on your chest, he hooks his left leg around yours and pushes, you fall flat on your back and he drops to one knee beside you, simultaneously chopping his right hand down onto your chest with a shout of Inner Force, cracking your ribs. Lose 11 Endurance. If you are still alive, you realise that you have only seconds before Yaemon finishes you, and the fear of death gives you the strength to roll aside and out of his reach. As quick as you can, you spring to your feet but he is upon you again with a flurry of attacks. If you have Acrobatics, turn to **181**. If not you must try and block. Your Defence is only 6, as you are still slightly stunned. If you succeed, turn to **118**. If you fail, turn to **308**.

151

The Grandmaster smiles and shakes his head. 'You have answered truthfully. It is not wrong that you should wish to avenge Naijishi, who loved you and taught you to love our Lord Kwon, but you must wait patiently for your time to come and never forget that the service of Kwon is the helping of all mankind. But as for torture, it is only through failing a mission that a true Ninja could be captured and there is always time to bite one's tongue from one's head and bleed to death rather than risk betraying secrets. You need only fear the failure of a mission. I shall not say that you have failed, for never has one mastered the Way of the Tiger so ably as you and we would not keep our sharpest weapon forever sheathed. You have passed the test.'

They lead you back to the Temple Hall where the monks and villagers have waited to see whether you would pass the test. Prayers to Kwon are offered up as part of the ceremony at which you are ordained as Grandmaster of the Five Winds. Gorobei applauds with the others, for now he remains an Adept of the Inner Circle but his time will come for he is a great warrior and a good monk. Should you die, he will probably succeed you. Turn to **191**.

152

The bolt of lightning catches you in the side, charring your flesh and jolting you as if you had been hit by a battering ram and you are sent hurtling to the far wall. Lose 8 Endurance. However, if you are still alive, you flip in the air and land safely on your feet. You manage to overcome the pain as the Barbarian moves to attack you with his longsword. Runeweaver leaps to your aid. The Barbarian concentrates his attacks on you, but you may roll an attack for Runeweaver against Olvar whenever you make a punch, kick or throw. Runeweaver does 1 Die + 1 Damage with his sword and Olvar's Defence against him is 8. You may use the Cobra Strike (turn to **92**), the Winged Horse kick (turn to **23**), the Dragon's Tail throw (turn to **39**) or, if you are skilled with Poison Needles, you may wish to use one (turn to **106**).

153

It is the work of a few moments to pick the lock with a small file. It clicks quietly and the well-oiled hinges make no sound as you open the cabin door. Inside the buccaneer Captain is sleeping, having forsaken his own cabin for the comfort of the Aquamarin. He is snoring heavily, dead drunk. Taking your time, you smear poison on the lockpick before jabbing it into his jugular vein. Turning, you shout the signal for the crew to break out as the Reaver Captain is wracked by death spasms. You lead the attack and the rum-sodden pirates are taken by surprise. Many jump into the sea, forgetting that their ship is a mile away in darkness. You are glad to see Glaivas, freed by one of the crew, despatching an ugly pirate who was proving troublesome. The few remaining alive surrender to him and he orders them put to the oar, for a taste of their own medicine. In the morning, you set sail again and make good speed. Turn to **26**.

154

The oak door grates slightly on its hinges as you enter Honoric's chamber. The fumes of poison curl like a snake from his mouth, and, overcoming the fear that emanates from the black blade, you grab it and leave the chamber as quickly as you can, taking care not to breathe until you are safely outside. You tie the great sword to your back and climb out of the turret window. Which turret will you climb to now? That which flies the flag of the Scarlet Mantis (turn to **361**) or the one that boasts the Black Whirlpool banner (turn to **141**)?

155

You face him sideways on, legs apart, knees slightly bent and your fists poised. Will you try the Cobra Strike punch (turn to **340**), the Iron Fist punch (turn to **330**) or the Tiger's Paw chop (turn to **410**) as he closes with you? You must decide now whether or not to use Inner Force, if you have any left.

156

You skirt the castle until you are an unseen shadow in the darkness below the derelict northern tower. You can see that the cracks which have appeared due to the subsidence of its foundations will make it easy to climb to one of its windows, but above the croaking of bullfrogs you can hear the pacing of guards somewhere within. You ease yourself soundlessly into the chill moat as the rain thrashes the surface around you. The noise of the bullfrogs is surprisingly loud and it is noticeable when they stop their croaking suddenly. Do you have some Essence of Firenewt? If so, turn to **147**, if not, turn to **132**.

157

The blow is so heavy that it sweeps through your guard and catches you on the side of the head. Lose 10 Endurance. If you are still alive, the pain is terrible as you fold to the ground. If you are able to slow your metabolism and Feign Death, you may turn to **376**. If you cannot or will not you pick yourself up and stagger towards the river. Turn to **103**.

158

You unfurl the length of waxed string until it dangles just above the mouth of the Marshal of the Legion of Doom. You uncork the gourd which holds the Blood of Nil, mouth of the Void, the most virulent poison known. It steams as the black beads run down the string and drop into Honoric's open mouth. He goes rigid and you know that he is helpless, dying of suffocation as his chest is paralysed. You have assassinated the Marshal of the Legion of Doom, one of the most powerful men on Orb. Turn to **305**.

159

The force of his throw sends you head over heels through the air and you crash to the ground on your back, stunned. An instant later, Yaemon has dropped to one knee beside you and he drives one fist and then the other in quick succession at your temple, giving a shout as he unleashes his Inner Force. Your skull cracks and you die instantly.

160

The white-furred giant swoops to sweep you to the ground with its great curved talons. You drive your fist towards its groin.

SNOW GIANT
Defence against Punch: 5
Endurance: 22
Damage: 1 Die + 3

If you have killed the Snow Giant turn to **111**. If the Snow Giant is still alive his talons rake at your face. Your Defence against this great sweep of his arm as you fight for your balance on the ice is 6. If you are still alive you may use the Forked Lightning Strike kick (turn to **184**), slide beneath his flailing arms and use the Dragon's Tail throw (turn to **202**) or punch again (return to top of this paragraph).

161

The Shuriken, enchanted by the priest of Fate, shrieks like a banshee as it hurtles towards the chest of the Elemental Being. It embeds itself and the Efreet becomes a pillar of flame, before disappearing. You have banished it to its home, the City of Brass. The Enchanted Shuriken has been taken to the elemental plane of fire, cross it off your Character Sheet. Shaking your head at your narrow escape, you journey on towards the Mountains of Vision. If you now wish to head west and then cross the Mountains of Vision at the Storm Giant's Causeway turn to **81**. Or if you would prefer to follow the winding river Fortune up into Fortune Pass and cross the mountains that way turn to **70**.

162

When you tell the guard in the castle gatehouse that you are a minstrel and juggler he says that there is to be a banquet tomorrow night for honoured guests, and asks you where you last performed. Do you reply:

'Ionalbion' (turn to **104**)?
'Mortavalon' (turn to **354**)?
'Druath Glennan' (turn to **124**)?

163

The mace rings on your iron sleeves like a hammer on the anvil and you grab your attacker's wrist, dragging him from the saddle. He falls awkwardly and rolls aside dead. The three others dismount and they begin to chant. They must be priests, you think. Will you attack them (turn to **96**) or run (turn to **103**)?

164

The spinning Shuriken takes the pirate Captain in the throat and the shout which was on his lips dies to a bloody gurgle as he slumps lifeless to the planks. You shout the signal and the crew rush up from the oar deck whirling lengths of chain and the cutlasses of their guards. You lead the attack and the rum-sodden pirates are taken by surprise. Many jump into the sea, forgetting that their ship is a mile away in darkness. You are glad to see Glaivas, freed by one of the crew, despatching an ugly pirate who was proving troublesome. The few remaining alive surrender to him and he orders them put to the oar, for a taste of their own medicine. In the morning, you set sail again and make good speed. Turn to **26**.

165

The bolt of lightning lances past you and sets the planks of the hut smouldering and, with Runeweaver, you attack. The Barbarian concentrates his attacks on you. You may roll an attack for Runeweaver whenever you make a punch, kick or throw. Olvar's Defence against Runeweaver is 8, and Runeweaver's sword does 1 Die + 1 Damage. Will you attack the Barbarian with a Cobra Strike to his unprotected neck (turn to **92**), employ the Winged Horse kick (turn to **23**), the Dragon's Tail throw (turn to **39**)? Or, if you are skilled with Poison Needles, you may wish to use one (turn to **106**).

166

You spend the next day in lonely vigil, but no-one leaves the castle, it is still a tenday before the moon will turn red at the conjunction of the planets and you can see preparations begin in the Outer Bailey. Yaemon, Honoric and Manse the Deathmage will set out for the Pillars of Change on the morrow. Your prayers to Kwon for a stormy moonless night are answered and you decide that on this night you will complete your mission or die honourably in the attempt. The wind and the rain and the darkness will make it possible for you to pass into the castle as if invisible. You prepare yourself in silent meditation, and don your ninja costume before staring up into the darkness until your night vision is as acute as an owl's. If you have the skill of Climbing and wish to scale the castle wall, turn to **392**. Alternatively, you may try the easy climb in through the derelict tower, whether or not you have the Climbing skill (turn to **156**). Otherwise, you may raise the grille outside the moat and drop to the tunnel below (turn to **402**).

167

You hurtle through the air to the ground and roll. Coming up on your feet, you flip forwards head over heels into the air and twist, so that you land facing Yaemon, who is springing to his feet. Seizing your chance, you cartwheel some way towards him, and then, turn into a head over heel flip to bring yourself within range, taking Yaemon by surprise.

Will you try a punch (turn to 266), a kick (turn to 390) or a throw (turn to 401)?

168

You step towards the monks. One of them sends the Toy-maker tumbling to the ground with a deft jab to the stomach as you demand that they cease tormenting him. He attacks with blinding speed, while you are looking to see if the Toy-maker is badly wounded. Your Defence against his sudden kick is 6. If he hits you he will do 1 Die + 2 Damage. If you are still alive, the monk steps back; they move with the grace of well-trained fighters. Confident of success, they decide to take you on one at a time. The one who kicked, steps forward and bows, as you do. Will you use the Tiger's Paw chop (turn to 322),

106

the Forked Lightning Strike kick (turn to **335**) or the Teeth of the Tiger throw (turn to **312**)?

169

You stroll through the arch and bid good-day to the labourers. As you walk on through the quiet streets of this dead city your heart is lightened by the sight of a rose garden and trees. You turn into the bower and find a small monastery dedicated to Kwon. Happy to find a safe haven where you may meditate and seek help you walk into the temple, and kneel at prayer. A monk kneels at your side in the bare temple and intones the psalm of Kwon the Redeemer. Turn to **221**.

170

You cannot miss the bulk of the Efreet and the throwing star embeds itself into its chest, where it begins, slowly, to melt. You will, of course, be unable to retrieve it. It has hurt the Elemental Being however, and you may subtract 2 from the Efreet's Endurance when you give battle. Turn to **149**.

171

As the first mailed man charges, swinging his mace down at you, you try to sweep the heavy mace aside with your forearm. Your Defence for this block is 8. If you succeed, turn to **163**. If you fail, turn to **157**.

172

You leap into the slimy green swamp and sink nearly to the waist. The bog sucks at your feet as you fight your way towards the boat which rocks gently in the middle of the morass of mud and slime. The Dark Elf is also bent on gaining the boat, but there is

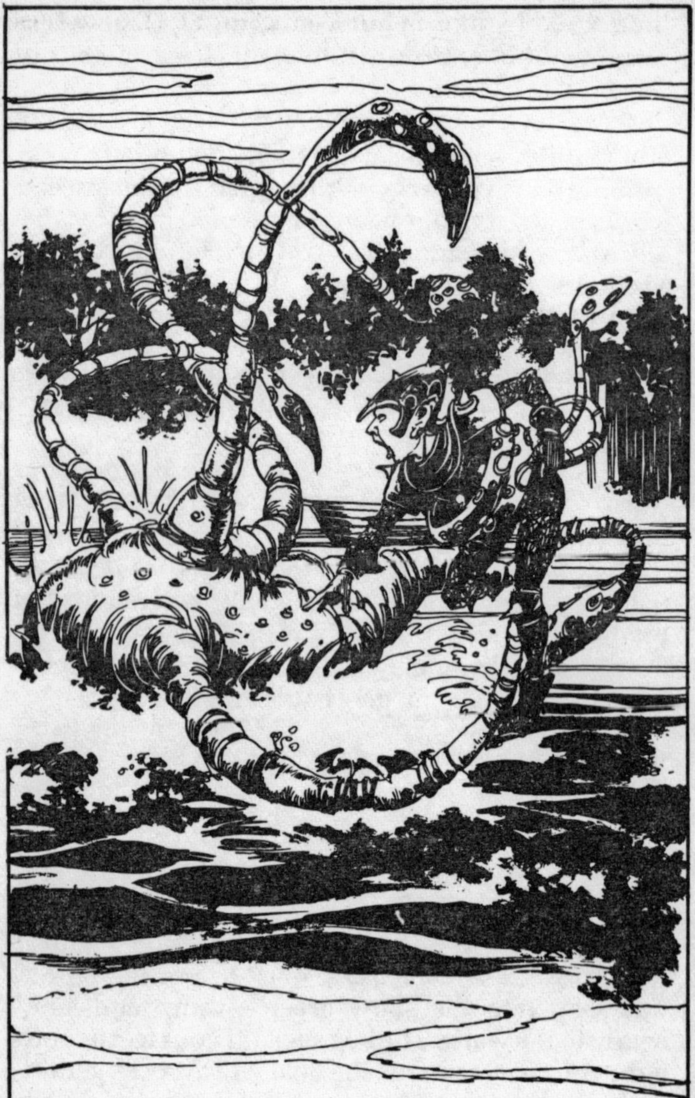

a sudden eruption of mud and slime as a featureless mass of blubber and threshing tentacles surges out of the water before her. It is a Shaggoth or slime beast, which wraps its stinking tentacles around the shrieking Dark Elf. You briefly catch sight of the desert, where the knight is battling the Cobra Man.

Will you:

Go to the aid of the Dark Elf (Turn to **98**)?
Make a grab for the boat (Turn to **121**)?
Wade on past and drag yourself out into the desert (Turn to **134**)?

173

Make a Fate Roll. If Fortune turns her back on you turn to **143**. If Fate smiles on you the climb is arduous but, apart from the moment when a small ledge of rock crumbles under your foot, uneventful. At last the wall of rock gives way to the entrance of a cave. Turn to **83**.

174

You climb like a spider up the wall of the Great Keep, flattening yourself against the stones, clinging motionless each time the guard, walking his rounds of the Inner Bailey, is below you. The wind and the rain cover the faint scraping of your Cat's Claws as you bury them in the loose mortar that holds the stones together, and you are invisible in the darkness. At last you are at the battlements and you peep out over the flat roof of the Keep. The three turrets, surprisingly large now that you are so close, still boast their flags which are faintly illuminated by the glow of a charcoal brazier. With his back to this stove is the Captain of the Guard, clad in black armour. Every now and then he patrols the battlements from one turret to another, before returning to warm himself at the brazier. He has taken his helmet off and is standing in the glow of the charcoals. Will you wait till he is beside the low battlements and attempt to throw him over the side (turn to **331**), use a Shuriken, aiming at his head (turn to **269**), creep up behind him and use your Garotte-wire (turn to **247**) or if you are skilled with Poison Needles will you use one (turn to **230**)?

175

The Captain shouts for help as the Shuriken is caught in the blankets and he throws them at you as you leap to attack. You cast them aside and duck a cutlass swipe before hearing a sound behind you. You whirl and block but are too late to catch the throwing knife of the Reaver's first mate. It lodges in your heart and you know no more.

176

You pay no attention but the insults continue and soon half of the soldiers in the room are shouting at you to fight. You decide that it is wise to leave the tavern and stride towards the door. The drunken young Captain lurches to his feet and draws his sword. It seems to glow as it leaves its sheath and a pall of fear descends upon you. You stop, the hairs bristling on your scalp. Grimly, you recite the Ninja Covenant, the Ninja No Chigiri, under your breath and courage returns. You move towards the door but the Captain and two of his friends decide to attack you with their swords. You must defend

111

yourself. Will you use the Winged Horse kick (turn to **256**), the Iron Fist punch (turn to **248**) or the Whirlpool throw (turn to **237**)?

177

The Grandmaster of the Dawn smiles and says, 'You pass the test for you have answered both truthfully and rightly. It is not wrong that you should wish to avenge Naijishi who loved you and taught you to love our Lord Kwon but you must wait patiently for your time to come and never forget that the service of Kwon is the helping of all mankind. It is only through failing a mission that a true Ninja would be captured and there is always time to bite off one's tongue from one's head and bleed to death rather than risk betraying secrets under torture.' He continues, 'We have never seen one who shows such promise nor one who has mastered so ably the Way of the Tiger. I am going to recite to you the secret litany of the Ninja Grandmaster – remember it, for one day it may be of use to you.

> I AM NINJA
> My parents are the Heaven and the Earth
> My Home is my Body
> My Power is Loyalty
> My Magic is Training
> My Life and my Death is Breathing
> My Body is Control
> My Eyes are the Sun and the Moon
> My Ears are Sensitivity
> My Laws are Self-Protection
> My Strength is Adaptability
> My Ambition is taking every Opportunity with Fullness

My Friend is my Mind
My Enemy is Carelessness
My Protection is Right Action
My Weapons are Everything that Exists
My Strategy is One Foot in front of the Other
My Trust is in Kwon
   MY WAY IS THE WAY OF THE TIGER'

His words are etched in your memory. Note this paragraph number down so that you can refer to the Litany again if you should need to do so.

Next, he pulls an Opal Ring from his finger and passes it to you. 'This may be of use to you,' he says and you slip it onto your own finger. When the echoing words of the Grandmaster have died away they lead you back to the Temple Hall where the monks and villagers have waited to see whether you would pass the test. Prayers to Kwon are offered up as part of the ceremony at which you are ordained as a Grandmaster of the Five Winds. Gorobei applauds with the others. For now he remains an Adept of the Inner Circle but his time will come, for he is a great warrior and a good monk. Should you die he will probably take your place. Turn to **191**.

178

The Captain ducks but he is too late, gurgling helplessly as you draw the wire ever tighter until it slices through his windpipe, before lowering his corpse gently to the floor. You notice that each of the three turrets has an archway leading to a spiral staircase.

Which turret will you climb?

The turret flying the Sword of Doom flag? Turn to **320**.

The turret flying the Scarlet Mantis flag? Turn to **148**.

The turret flying the Black Whirlpool flag? Turn to **130**.

179

On your way to Quench-heart Keep, you come across the tracks of three horses and a camp. You quicken your pace, hoping to catch them before they gain the safety of the castle. Following the tracks across the Wold leads you towards the Goblin's Teeth Mountains, jagged and black, and before them stands a great castle, built out of the same sombre stone. The gatehouse is flanked by two stout posts which have been driven into the ground. Two Iron-maidens, metal cages lined with spikes, in the shape of a sarcophagus, sway gently in the wind. The corpse inside one is shrunken and rotted but the other holds an emaciated man whose beard and hair have grown down to his waist. He is too mad even to plead for help from strangers. Three horsemen enter the gatehouse some way ahead of you, a man in a scarlet robe flanked by two men in black, both tall but one is thin where the other is built like a bear. For the first time you have sighted your quarry.

The Great Keep itself rises high above the walls, surmounted by three towers, each of which flies a banner. The most northerly boasts a Scarlet Mantis, the west tower, a silver sword hanging by a needle thread, the Sword of Doom and the third the black whirlpool symbol of Nemesis.

As you approach the gatehouse, two soldiers drag a screaming man to a grille outside the moat.

'Feeding time,' says one and they laugh as they raise

the grille and throw their prisoner down to whatever lurks in the castle dungeons.

Will you wait for dark before trying to enter the castle (turn to **145**) or try to pass yourself off as a minstrel, one of the Seven Ways of Going, so that you can reconnoitre the castle first (turn to **162**)?

180

As you place the needle in your mouth the Efreet spreads its arms. You blow hard and the needle sinks into the Efreet's flesh but is consumed by flames which lick across its body. It has no effect. Before you can move, flames leap from its open arms and you are encircled by fire. You are held powerless in its arms and the world of Orb fades to greyness around you. You writhe in the Efreet's burning embrace as you see a new landscape appearing around you. Brazen castles and walls hem you in and a dirgeful braying of horns heralds your arrival at the City of Brass. The brass floor is so hot that it blisters your feet and you know of no way to leave the Elemental Plane of Fire. Your quest ends here.

181

You leap high to the side and, cartwheeling in the air, land some feet beyond Yaemon, just as he was about to chop at you. Somewhat surprised by your athletic powers, he turns to face you, as you flip towards him, head over heels several times, and leap to the attack. Will you punch (turn to **266**), kick (turn to **390**) or try and throw him (turn to **401**)?

182

You crouch on the ground and the horses thunder over you. Turn to **135**.

183

The priest replies, 'Even if we were not busy with healing we would not help you, for those who follow the strict laws of a monastery, as you must, hinder freedom and prevent paradise on Orb.' You realise from the look of zeal in his eyes that theological argument would not sway him. Will you:

Tell him of your quest and ask for his help again (turn to **297**)?

Leave the temple and the Sanctuary and pass through the Obsidian Gate into Doomover (turn to **6**)?

184

You lash your left foot at the great mould of white fur twice in quick succession, aiming for its side and temple, but almost lose your footing. Make a Fate Roll. If Fate smiles on you read on, but if Fate turns her back on you turn to **146**.

SNOW GIANT
Defence against Forked Lightning Strike: 6
Endurance: 22
Damage: 1 Die + 3

If you have killed the Snow Giant turn to **111**. Otherwise the Snow Giant tries to crush you with a swipe from its taloned claw. Your Defence as you strive to keep your balance on the ice is 5. If you are still alive you may slide beneath its flailing arms and use the Dragon's Tail throw (turn to **202**), use the Iron Fist punch (turn to **160**) or kick again (return to the top of this paragraph).

185

You walk on down the main street, the Dreamer's Saunter and turn right onto Wheel Way. The city seems tranquil until you hear raised voices ahead. Two men, wearing brown habits which bear the symbol of the cross of Avatar upside down with a serpent writhing in mist atop it, are cruelly taunting a puppet-maker. A small girl is crying but other townsfolk pass by on the other side of the road, staring straight ahead. The two men are forcing him to open his mouth and then while one holds his head, the other is trying to shove glove puppets down his throat. From the symbol you recognise these men as Reverencers of Vile. Will you step in and try to save the Toy-maker (turn to **168**) or ignore the incident leaving him to his fate (turn to **299**)?

186

The young soldier sneers and calls you a plague-ridden sewer rat. You sit in a corner, ignoring him. Your heightened sense of hearing enables you to eavesdrop on their conversation rather than the countless others in the crowded tavern. It seems they are waiting for the leader of the Legion of the Sword of Doom, Honoric, to return before they march against the Spires of Foreshadowing. It seems he has left the city with Yaemon, heading north. One of the drunken soldiers at the next table starts to insult you and then tells you that if you want to live you should leave the tavern now. Will you stay in your seat (turn to **176**) or take a room upstairs for the night (turn to **225**)?

187

As the dust enters the flames there is a brilliant flash. You had shaded your eyes, but Olvar and

Runeweaver are, for the moment, blinded. The Barbarian backs out of the doorway and you follow up with a flying Winged Horse to his chest and he throws his arms up and crashes backwards into the snow. Note that he has lost 5 Endurance, for you have cracked some of his ribs. You are about to run out into the snow to finish him, when a bolt of blue lightning discharges from the gem at his forehead towards the doorway. You try to duck back inside and your Defence against the Lightning bolt is 6, as Olvar's sight returns. If you manage to dodge, turn to **127**. If you fail to dodge, turn to **142**.

188
With the speed of a cobra you chop both hands across the path of the twin crossbow bolts, crossing them in front of your chest and the bolts hurtle to the walls on either side of you. You move silently to the spiral staircase and wait to check that no one has heard the clattering of the iron bolts. Satisfied, you glide up the staircase. Turn to **399**.

189
Even in the difficult conditions of darkness, wind and rain, the light from the brazier is enough for you to tear the Captain's throat out with your Shuriken, at a range of thirty feet. He collapses with a clatter of armour but his cry of pain was strangled at its source. Each of the three turrets has an archway leading to a spiral staircase. Which turret will you climb:

The one flying the Sword of Doom flag? Turn to **320**.
The one flying the Scarlet Mantis? Turn to **148**.
The one flying the Black Whirlpool? Turn to **130**.

190

The floorboards come up easily, revealing black dirt below. There is a layer of breathable air at floor level, below the smoke and you set to work burrowing into the earth. When you have made a hole large enough to crouch in, you cover yourself with earth, poking your breathing tube through it for what little air you can get, using your control of breathing to minimize your needs. You sweat and gasp for breath but the soil protects you from the fire, which dies away when it has consumed the wooden room. You lie still as a party of monks come to investigate. It seems they had ringed the place waiting for you to emerge but now they think you are dead. You overhear them talking about the imminent arrival at Quench-heart Keep of Yaemon, accompanied by Honoric of the Legion of the Sword of Doom and Manse the Deathmage, a most powerful sorcerer and a follower of Nemesis, the Supreme Principle of Evil, and how they will be pleased that you are dead. When they have left, you leave your hole and take the road past the Hydra's Heads Inn out of the city and towards the Goblin's Teeth Mountains before which lies Quench-heart Keep. Turn to **179**.

191

After the ceremony you all file out of the temple onto the golden sands and there is a frugal feast of rice and fruits shared by the villagers and the monks. You eat sparingly and take your leave early, wishing to meditate before you sleep. Relaxed from the meditation which frees your spirit from the shackles of your aching body your eyes close as soon as you lay yourself down on the straw-filled sacking that is your bed. You drift into a deep but troubled sleep. You see a sleek-oared ship setting sail from the Land of Plenty. A tall resolute looking man is on the high stern castle, his legs braced against the swell. He wears a thick cloak of dark green against the weather and the sun flashes so vividly on the buckle of his sword belt that you believe this is not a dream but a vision. A sailor calls him by name, 'Glaivas', and he turns to look at you but then the vision fades and the brilliant blue sky is replaced by sombre purple clouds against which a large and dark castle looms. Three turrets on a great black Keep seem to pierce the clouds. You are walking towards it, bent on completing a difficult and important mission.

When you awake you remember the dreams as if they were pictures painted on the wall of your monastic cell, but your sleep has at least restored any Endurance you lost in your contest with Gorobei. You are walking towards the Temple when there is a commotion on the beach and two fishermen run up to you with the news that a ship is riding at anchor offshore. A man rows himself to the beach and steps out, as the Grandmasters walk to the strand to greet him. He introduces himself as Glaivas and, bowing respectfully, he asks to talk to the Grandmaster of Grandmasters.

'You may address us all,' says the Grandmaster of the Dawn, 'for we have no secrets on the Island of Tranquil Dreams.'

'Not since you lost the Scrolls of Kettsuin,' Glaivas returns darkly.

'What do you know of the Scrolls of Kettsuin?', asks the Grandmaster. The monks wait tensely as Glaivas looks around carefully before replying.

'The Scrolls of Kettsuin hold the secret to the Word of Power which will bind Kwon himself in Inferno if it is spoken at the Pillars of Change in the great snow-wastes of the north. Yaemon, Grandmaster of Flame, of the order of the Scarlet Mantis stole it from you many years ago and he has deciphered the Word. It is the month of All-Mother Splendour and for three days the moon will turn red during the Great Conjunction of the Planets – something that occurs only once every five hundred years. If the Word is spoken by the Pillars of Change at this time your God, Kwon, will be imprisoned in the bottomless pit of fire, leaving the monks who worship Vile free to spread their dominion over the lands of men.'

At the mention of Yaemon's name there is uproar but as Glaivas continues an unnatural quiet descends.

'Yaemon is preparing to set out even now from the city of Doomover on the long journey to the Ice Wastes. Though a Ranger long used to patrolling the wilderness on the edge of the Rift, I am no match for such as he. Is there one among you who will try to stop him?'

As Glaivas spoke you felt the burning need to be

revenged on Yaemon flare within your breast. Your dream of Glaivas, for it was he you saw astride the deck of the ship which now rides at anchor near the sands, has convinced you that you are destined for this quest and you step forward saying, 'I shall stop him.'

'You are young,' says Glaivas, 'can you succeed where I, a Ranger Lord, would fail?'

'I am Ninja,' you reply.

Glaivas starts. The Grandmaster of the Dawn sighs and says, 'Yes, I rename you Avenger, for if anyone can succeed, and you must for the sake of all mankind, it will be you.' With that he turns towards the Temple, and prayer.

The city of Doomover lies on the western coast of the Manmarch and Glaivas gifts you a map which shows the many cities and strange lands which stretch north to the snow wastes. You spend the rest of the day preparing, lacing the iron sleeves to your dark hued costume and gathering together the tools of the Ninja, before spending some hours in quiet meditation. You board Glaivas' ship in time to sail on the evening tide. You must find Yaemon and kill him before he reaches the Pillars of Change or all will be lost. Turn to **232**.

192

As the lions charge you, you make the most incredible leap; the crowd gasps as you somersault over them and then sprint for the swamp. They check and turn with startling speed and you reach the murky green just as the lions are snapping at your heels, but they pull up, fearing to jump into the unnatural greenness of the slime-covered water. Turn to **172**.

193
You fix the Cat's Claws to your hands and climb carefully up the rock face, avoiding any ledges where cracks warn you that the rock may crumble beneath you. At length the sheer rock-face gives way to a cave mouth. Turn to **83**.

194
You sit at his table and he calls for a hogshead of mead. He smiles at you, lids lowered, as the mead arrives and he plunges two mugs into the brimming bucket and places one carefully before you. You raise the mugs together and drain them. There is a cheer as you slam the mugs back down together. The young captain dips them into the bucket again and again a cheer answers your efforts. Do you have Immunity to Poisons? If you do, turn to **214**. If you do not, turn to **206**.

195
You sidestep the swinging mace and spring up

behind the mailed man, landing on his horse. The horse rears and you try to chop him to the ground as he twists in the saddle to mace your face. His Defence against your Tiger's Paw is 5. If your blow lands, turn to **387**. If you fail to hit him, turn to **407**.

196

You walk up the steps and into the Temple. The wooden pews seem to be placed at random within, but the roof is pierced with rose-windows and the inside is bright and cheerful. Crystals reflect the sun's rays against a painting showing a demolished castle, and soldiers and peasants dancing in the meadows before it. There is no sign of the decapitated priest or the young warrior. One of the priests walks towards you and you ask him if he can help you with some information. He asks you whether you are a worshipper of Béatan. Which god will you say you worship? Kwon (turn to **183**), the Allmother (turn to **46**) or Béatan (turn to **56**) or would you rather hasten from the Temple to follow the old man who called himself a Seer (turn to **36**)?

197

You have defeated the Elemental Being and you step back as the Efreet becomes a pillar of flame, before disappearing. You have banished it to its home, the City of Brass. If you wish to head west and then cross the Mountains of Vision at the Storm Giant's Causeway, turn to **81**. Or if you would prefer to follow the winding river Fortune up into Fortune Pass and cross the mountains that way, turn to **70**.

198

Two crossbow bolts discharge from a trap in the wall

and one of them pierces your windpipe. You sink gurgling to the floor and your lungs fill with blood. You drown in your own life-blood in the hallway of Quench-heart Keep.

199

It is a difficult throw at this range, in the wind and swirling rain, at a target lit only by the charcoal brazier. The throwing star clangs as it penetrates the armour on his back, but the Captain's wound is only a light one. He shouts the alarm as you close to attack and he moves behind the brazier which he throws over. You leap above the glowing coals as a black-robed figure appears in the air above you. It is Manse the Deathmage and you dimly see the twisted smile on his face as he casts a spell which sends you into a helpless shaking fit. Honoric bursts from the archway of his turret and you are helpless as the Marshal of the Legion of the Sword of Doom snatches the sword from the Captain's hand and cuts your head cleanly from your shoulders.

200

You step through the doorway of the Volunteer Inn and are surprised to see a wheel-shaped room, airy and light with a circular bar at its centre. There are ten tables with chairs screwed into the floor around them but perhaps because of the sound the door makes, everyone seems to be looking at you, and all conversation ceases. A man dressed in robes which bear the symbol of a ten-spoked wheel greets you as Avenger and invites you to join him. You sit opposite him and demand how he knows your name.

He replies, 'We who follow Fate may often know what will come to pass. Our leader, Whimsical, foresees the arrival of all strangers.'

'But surely,' you ask, 'with such power he could rule the Manmarch?'

'We only see what we are fated to see and it is not Whimsical's fate to rule the Manmarch.'

You tell him that there is a conspiracy amongst the followers of evil gods to enslave their fellow men. The priest replies that he knows this and when you demand what the followers of Fate plan to do, he merely spreads his hands and says, 'What will be, will be, and you cannot change it.' He goes on, however, to say that he realises that the Spires of

Foreshadowing with its great cathedral to Fate will fall first if the evil ones have their way, and he says that he is on your side. He even asks you to become a Tool of Fate and to join the elite band of heroes who are fated to do great deeds in her service, and to embrace the worship of Fate.

'For she is above other gods, Keeper of the Balance, without which all things would perish.'

You have heard of the elite few who serve Fate as her Tools, this is indeed an honour. One of the drinkers leaves the Inn as he invites you to go with him to Fiendil's cathedral to Fate. Will you embrace the worship of Fate (turn to **100**) or politely decline the priest's offer (turn to **76**)?

201

You use the side of your hand to chop the quarrel aside before it hits you and then roll out of the torchlight. You lie low, motionless, until you hear a shout from a side street. 'Stop thief,' someone cries, as a man carrying a dagger runs into the torchlight. He squeals in fright as the gateguards charge after him and you slip unnoticed out of the city gate at the first ray of dawn. Turn to **65**.

202

The crowd gasp as you slide beneath the grasp of the white furred colossus and wrapping your legs around its, twist your body in an effort to throw it to the ground. Though surer-footed in these conditions than most, the Snow Giant still finds the ice slippery, but its legs are as wide as your chest.

SNOW GIANT
Defence against Dragon's Tail throw: 6
Endurance: 22
Damage: 1 Die + 3

If you have thrown the Snow Giant successfully you may either use the Forked Lightning Strike kick (turn to **184**) or the Iron Fist punch (turn to **160**), adding 3 to your Kick or Punch Modifier for this attack only, as you leap to your feet, ready to aim a blow as it struggles upwards. If you have failed to throw the Snow Giant, it tries to stamp on your head as you roll aside, trying to get to your feet as quickly as possible. Your Defence against this is 7, and you find yourself with no time to block. If you survive you may use the Forked Lightning Strike kick (turn to **184**) or the Iron Fist punch (turn to **160**).

203

The ring on your finger grows warm and, as you watch, the opal stone becomes clear and seems to grow. Looking into it you see a man's face; it is pallid and white, with a long, hooked nose and hollow cheeks. His large blood-red eyes are staring intently out of the opal, questing for something or someone. They narrow and his brow furrows with annoyance. He curses and you are shocked to hear his voice, resonant and macabre, as he says, 'I cannot see you, Follower, but know that none can stand before the sorcery of Manse the Deathmage.' With that he pulls back and behind him, you catch sight of another, a man in scarlet robes, with a belt of black and gold. It is Yaemon, Grandmaster of Flame. You press on, eager to catch up with them. If you wish to head west and then cross the Mountains of Vision at the Storm Giant's Causeway, turn to **81**. Or if you would prefer to follow the winding river Fortune up into Fortune Pass and cross the mountains that way, turn to **70**.

204
The Barbarian's eyes never leave yours as he takes the money pouch from you. Then, sneering, he demands your Ninja accoutrements as well. Rather than give away the equipment you need for your mission, you jump to the attack. A bolt of blue lightning discharges from the gem at Olvar's forehead, with a crack. Almost instantaneously, you try to twist aside. Your Defence against the lightning bolt as you try to dodge is 5. If you manage to dodge, turn to **406**. If you fail to dodge, turn to **85**.

205
Your costume catches fire as you leap through the flames and you cannot breathe, the fire is taking all of the oxygen. You collapse to the floor and the fire rages all around you. A falling beam mercifully releases you from the searing agony. When the fire dies there is nothing left of you but a blackened skeleton.

206
The barman had mixed Spirits-of-Ra into the mead and it was stronger than you realized. The alcohol passes into your bloodstream quickly and you stand up to leave but pass out. You wake up in the morning, lying muddied in the gutter. Some of your

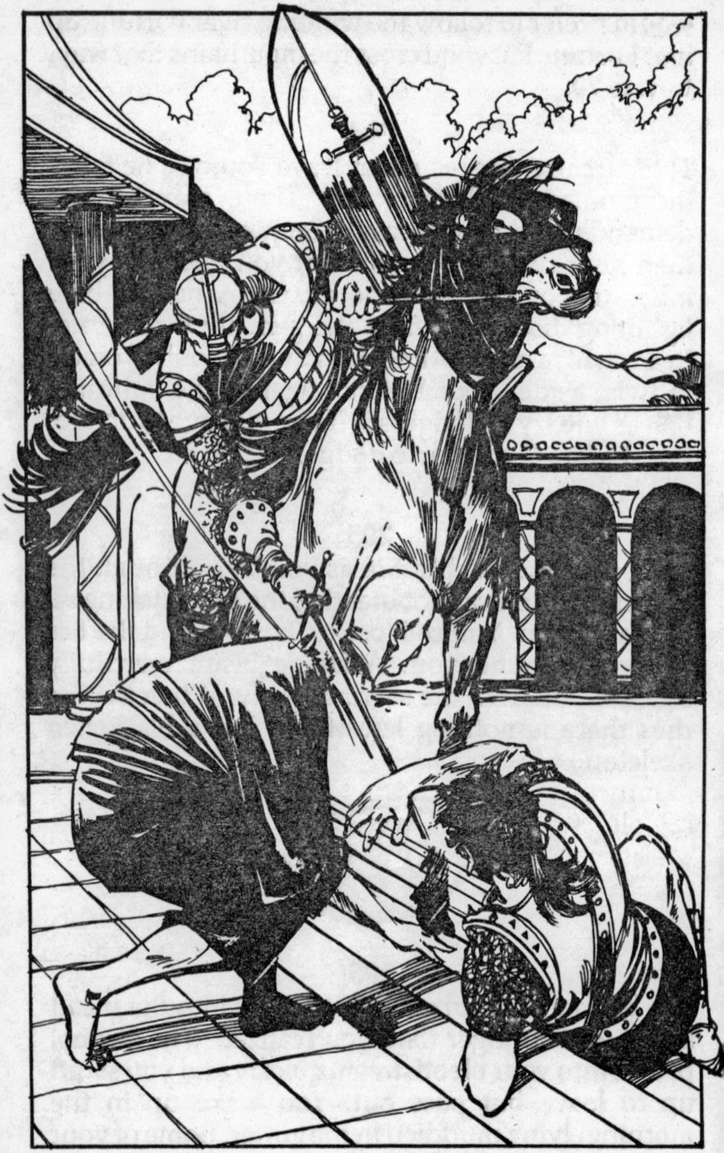

gold coins have been taken, but you had hidden five upon your person, which you still have. If you had an Opal ring, you notice that has also been stolen. Cross it off your Character Sheet. You decide to head north in case Yaemon arrives at the Pillars of Change before you, and leave the city on the road to Mortavalon. Turn to **65**.

207

You step towards the staircase, hoping to find your way to the turrets atop the Keep, but a flagstone settles slightly underfoot and there is a click from the wall to your right. Do you have the skill of Arrow Cutting? If you do, turn to **188**. If you do not have this skill, turn to **198**.

208

As you step between the pillars of white marble a voice speaks as if from the stones, 'Welcome to the Sanctuary, draw no swords here.' You can't see anyone nearby but ahead of you, a huge young warrior clad in russet and grey is crawling painfully up the steps of a temple. A priest in yellow robes comes out to help him but, as he leans down, a mounted knight in a black surcoat rides up the temple steps and lops the priest's head off. Another priest casts a spell, the horse rears backwards and then two other horsemen wearing the same coat of arms, a silver sword hanging by a silver thread on a black background, ride up and take the reins from their friend. He curses the young warrior in a rage but seems helpless as they lead him past you and gallop out through the marble gate. Priests carry their decapitated colleague and the young warrior, who has left a trail of blood on the steps, into the temple.

As they do so a wizened, stooped old man with a necklace of crystal which clicks as he sways, croaks, 'I foretold it but did you heed me, the Seer? No! Will Béatan the Free smile on you now, false priests?' He turns and shuffles towards a small wooden chapel. The dead priest served Béaten whose followers seek to bring nearer paradise on Orb by living lives of capricious goodness mocking all laws that constrict the free spirit. Do you:

Follow the priests into the temple of Béatan the Free (turn to **196**)?
Leave the Sanctuary and pass through the Obsidian Gate (turn to **6**)?
Follow the old man who claimed to be a Seer (turn to **36**)?

209

The Captain of the Guard ducks and drives his elbow back into your stomach. You leap back and he throws the brazier of coals onto the ground. You leap above the glowing coals as a black-robed figure appears in the air above you. It is Manse the Death-mage and you dimly see the twisted smile on his face as he casts a spell which sends you into a helpless shaking fit. Honoric bursts from the door of his turret and you are helpless as the Marshal of the Legion of the Sword of Doom snatches the sword from the Captain's hand and cuts your head cleanly from your shoulders.

210

On the morning of the third day out from Mortavalon you are high up in Fortune Pass, the air is crisp and scented with mountain heather. Mount Gwalodrun rises to a jagged peak before you. You climb up the scree slope at its base, slipping backwards whenever the pebbles avalanche, until you reach a belt of pines. At the tree line the mountain side becomes sheer and dangerous. If you are a skilled Climber, turn to 193; if you are not, turn to 133.

211

As they spring together you leap and kick, but they instinctively claw your foot aside. One smashes you to the ground and before you can roll out from underneath, it buries its teeth in your neck. The crowd howls in frenzied glee as the lions tear at you ferociously, and you welcome Death's embrace.

212

You trot along the road, passing the occasional traveller, on horseback or on foot, and an occasional

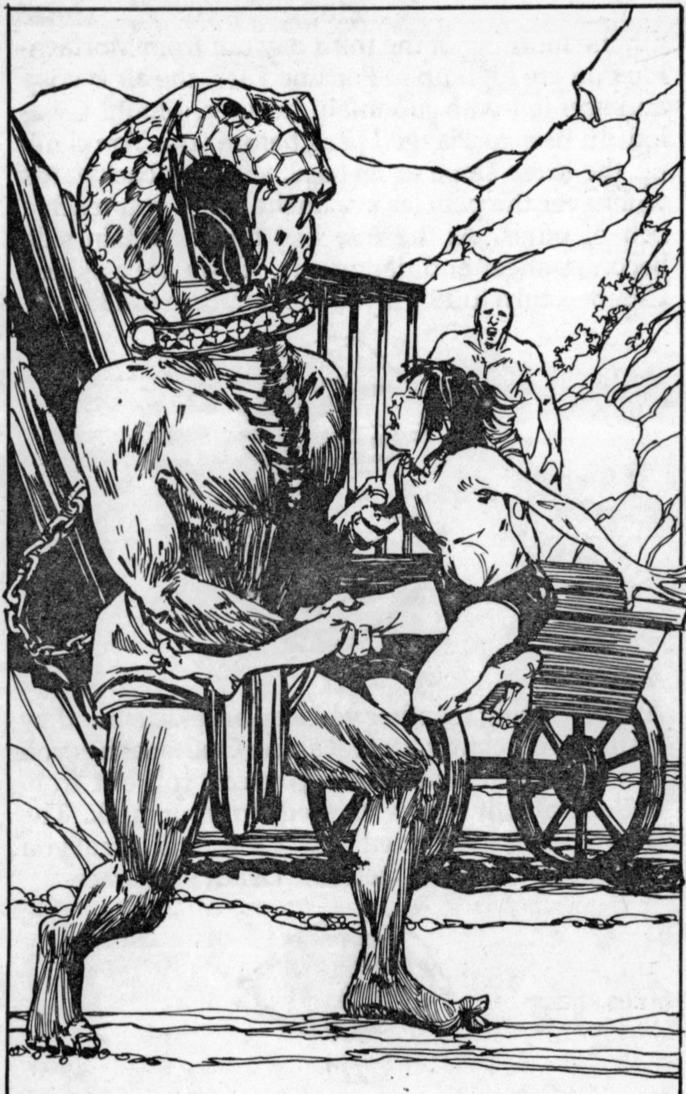

trading caravan, gathering berries and nuts at the side of the road as you go. You sleep away from the road. You may restore up to 2 Endurance and continue on, hoping to reach Mortavalon at dusk on the second day. The road winds upwards into a range of hills which encircle the city of Mortavalon, and it is afternoon when you hear a strange hissing and a sudden scream around a corner ahead. You move stealthily forwards to see a black-skinned man with the swaying neck and head of a cobra, tethered to a wagon on which there is a large cage. The Cobra Man has grabbed a young boy and is about to kill him. The two men who are on the wagon look too terrified to do anything. Will you leave the young boy to his fate (turn to **357**) or run and kick the Cobra Man (turn to **315**)?

213

As the crumbling walls of Fiendil are lost to sight behind you, a vague shimmering disturbs the air. You feel warmth on your face as a strange being takes shape before you. It is the size of a giant but its skin is ruby red and covered in running flames. Its wide grinning mouth is filled with curving yellow tusks and two yellow smoking horns crown its head. It speaks in a deep rumbling voice.

'My master, Manse the Deathmage, has sent me to take you to the City of Brass, in the Elemental Plane of Fire.'

Life in the dread City of Brass is worse than death itself. You may leap to attack the Efreet (turn to **149**), or, if you are skilled in the use of Poison Needles you may wish to use one (turn to **180**). However, you may wish to use a Shuriken. If you have an Enchanted Shuriken and wish to use it, turn to **161**. If you wish to use a normal Shuriken, turn to **170**.

214

Your training with the ingestion of small quantities of poisons also included large amounts of alcohol and you can drink almost anyone under the table. The young Captain begins slurring his words and the pace of drinking slows. You tell them that you are a monk who worships Vile and they treat you as one of them. The young Captain asks you about the journey that Honoric, leader of the Legion of the Sword of Doom, is making with Yaemon. You tell them that Yaemon is journeying north on important business. They laugh at this and begin to joke with you that Honoric's business is more important. You gather that he too knows a word which will bind a goddess in Inferno and that they are journeying to the Snow Wastes. After a time you pretend that you are overcome by the mead and take a room for the night in the tavern for which you pay 2 pieces of gold. You sleep lightly, senses alert, but are not disturbed. You wake in the morning, mildly refreshed. Restore 1 Endurance if you wish. You leave and walk out of the city on the road to Mortavalon. Turn to **65**.

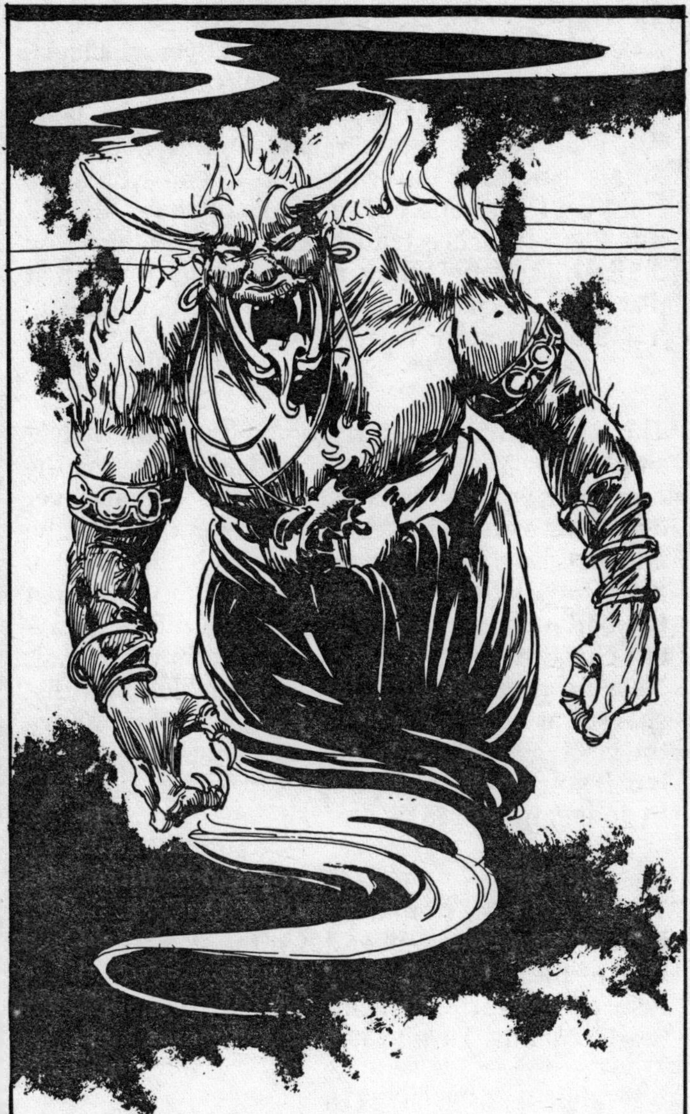

215

As you carefully inspect the ground over which you will tread on your way to the staircase which may lead up to the turrets, you notice that the large flagstone before you is raised slightly above the others. Scanning the walls around you, you see a crack outlining one of the blocks of stone. Edging this open reveals a twin-crossbow trap which you deftly disarm by lifting the iron bolts from their place, before crossing to the staircase. You glide up it without a sound. Turn to **399**.

216

The Barbarian's eyes dart from you to Runeweaver as he takes your money pouch. Then, sneering, he demands your Ninja tools as well. Runeweaver draws his sword and, cursing you for a coward, he attacks Olvar. Before he can close with him, a bolt of lightning discharges with a crack from the gem at the Barbarian's forehead. It slams into Runeweaver's chest and he is hurled against the far wall, dead. Next he turns on you and another blue bolt discharges at you. You try to leap straight up, above the lancing bolt. Your Defence against the lightning is 6. If you dodge successfully, turn to **406**. If you fail to dodge, turn to **85**.

217

You climb down from the attic and walk away from Honoric's death chamber down the staircase to the roof of the Great Keep below and climb the staircase of the turret which flies the banner of the Scarlet Mantis. Turn to **397**.

218

It is a difficult throw at this range, in the wind and

swirling rain, at a target lit only by the charcoal brazier. The throwing star whirs past his head and away, landing outside the castle walls. The Captain of the Guard has not noticed it. Will you wait till he is at the edge of the roof and throw him over (turn to **331**), use a poison needle if you have the skill to do so (turn to **230**), steal up behind and garotte him (turn to **247**) or wait until he comes closer and try again with another Shuriken? If you do throw again, make an Attack Roll.

If you score 7–12: Turn to **189**.
If you score 2–6: Turn to **199**.

219

The sea breeze carries the salt spray of the sea to you as you trot along the eastern coast of the Sea of the Star. To save time you decide to swim across the narrow eastern point of the star-shaped sea and the chill water is invigorating. At last you enter the narrow cobbled streets of the city of Druath Glennan. The houses are tall and thin, built of dark brick save for the wooden balconies which almost touch above, making the streets dark and gloomy. You are glad to have disguised yourself as a fisherman since the guards are unmistakedly in the pay of the monks who worship Vile. Their red-shuttered monastery runs along one side of the Square of the Gods, faced by a temple to the All-Mother. You notice a poor house in one of the dingy side streets and, changing into the guise of a beggar, you fall in with the drunkards who are supported there by the priestesses of the All-Mother. You are planning to reconnoitre the monastery to Vile, hoping that Yaemon is within, when you overhear one of the beggars telling the story of how he lost his arm. There is a grimy and bloody bandage hanging loosely from his shoulder. It seems he was once a sweeper in the monastery but was thrown out because of his drinking. Hearing through the grapevine that Yaemon, Grandmaster of Flame, was visiting the monastery, he foolishly decided to throw himself before the arch monk and beg for his job again. Yaemon, surprisingly, received him but sneeringly told him that even the gutter was too good a place for him. He had a friend with him, 'a wicked looking man, with a wicked heart. He had the most hideous, soulless red eyes . . . Manse the Deathmage, they called him. Anyway, just for sport he said he would punish me, and before I know it my arm drops off. I would have bled to death if it hadn't been for the priestesses.'

He gets little sympathy; one of them, his voice slurred by drink, asks him what he expects if he mixes with Yaemon, Grandmaster of Flame, and the Deathmage, the most powerful sorcerer on Orb. You gather from their conversation that Yaemon had been waiting with Honoric, leader of the Legion of the Sword of Doom, for Manse the Deathmage to join them in Druath Glennan. Now they have set out for a castle called Quench-heart Keep, near the

Goblins' Teeth Mountains. As it is now late, you decide to stay in the poor-house and set off in the morning.

You are awakened in the night by the smell of acrid smoke. The room in which you are sleeping is on fire and a sheet of flame blocks the doorway and fills the hallway beyond. There are no windows through which to escape. The room is filling with smoke. What will you do? Leap through the solid wall of flame (turn to **205**) or tear up the loose floorboards (turn to **190**)?

220

You run to the ice and leap onto it, sliding away from the lions. They charge after you but lose their footing on the treacherous surface, the look on their faces quite comical as they experience something completely unexpected. You manage to negotiate your way past them, using your excellent sense of balance. Each time they lunge for you their feet slip and they fall flat. You sprint across the plain and leap into the swamp. The lions, gaining the grass, again snap at your heels but pull up short at the edge of the unnaturally green slime. Turn to **172**.

221

As you meditate in the temple your body and soul seem filled with the harmony of Kwon the Redeemer. You may restore up to 3 points of Inner Force, as the God lends you his power. The monk, Bartholdy, recognises that you have the favour of Kwon and asks you to preach to his brothers in the refectory before dinner. You decline, telling him instead of your quest. Upon hearing that you are Ninja he agrees that only he and the local Grandmaster should know of your mission. The Grandmaster, Bartok, a frail old man, wise but weak, is filled with fear at your news. He has heard, however, that Yaemon has passed through Mortavalon eight days since, perhaps, he thinks, heading for the monastery of the Reverencers of Vile in the city of Fiendil. He advises that you strike north towards Fortune Pass, so that you may come to the lands of snow, before the Grandmaster of Flame. He continues, 'There is a man who lives in the mountains, a mystic, but a follower of the Way of the Tiger. He is older than I but, by the grace of Kwon, he has remained fit and strong. His name is Togawa and, long ago, he was the Grandmaster of the Dawn on the Island of Tranquil Dreams. He lives on Mount Gwalodrun and from there he sets his mind free to roam all the planes of existence. He may be able to tell you where you can find Yaemon.'

You dine alone in a small monkish cell and your sleep refreshes you. Restore up to four points of any lost Endurance. On the following day you leave the monks to prepare against the day of darkness, should you fail your mission. You have not caught up with Yaemon yet and so you leave the city through the northern arch in the morning. Will you

strike across the wastelands towards Fiendil (turn to
260), head due north to Storm Giants' Causeway
(turn to **81**) or head northeast to Fortune Pass and
the mystic, Togawa (turn to **210**)?

222

The monk's head jerks backwards, his skull distorted by the power of your blow. His neck breaks with a sound like a whip-crack and his head lolls foolishly, like the heads of the puppets made by the Toy-maker whose life you have saved. He is recovering and smiles his thanks, but the little girl, his daughter, runs up to you and smothers your hand in kisses. You ask the Toy-maker if he has seen Yaemon, a Grand Master of the order of the Scarlet Mantis. He shakes his head.

'No-one guards the gates here, there's no telling who comes and goes.' You thank him and, politely refusing his offer of hospitality, decide to leave Fiendil before the Reverencers of Vile find out what you have done to two of their brothers. Turn to **289**.

223

You jog along the road, passing a few travellers on horseback or on foot, and an occasional trading caravan, gathering berries and nuts at the side of the road as you go. You sleep away from the road. You may restore up to 2 Endurance and continue on, hoping to reach Mortavalon at dusk on the second day. Around mid-day another small caravan of four wagons, approaches. There are four caravan guards, on horseback, dressed in chain mail and, curiously, all carrying maces. You jog on, wary now, when suddenly, one of them cries, 'The Ninja!' and they charge towards you, swinging their

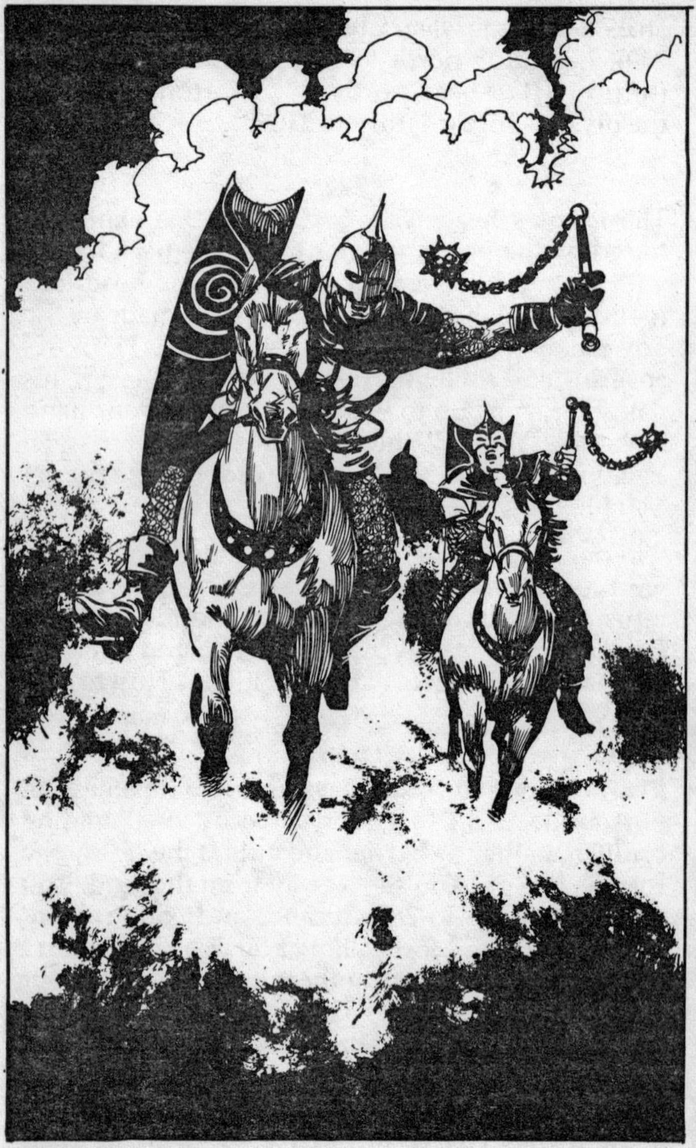

weapons. As they close, you see that they bear the black whirlpool symbol. If you are an Acrobat you may wish to try to dodge aside and leap up behind one of your attackers (turn to **195**). If not, will you Block the first mace blow with your iron sleeve and try to topple your assailant from the saddle (turn to **171**), or duck to the ground knowing that their horses will avoid trampling you (turn to **182**)?

224

The evil Torturer is thrown into the water by your killing blow, where he bobs gently, face downwards. The prisoners implore you to release them and, seizing the opportunity to create a diversion, you do so, asking only that they wait to the count of two hundred before following you out of the chamber. Turn to **270**.

225

You give the barman two pieces of gold for the room and go upstairs. You sleep lightly, senses alert and you are ready when three drunken soldiers burst in. It is the work of a few moments to knock two of them unconscious with deft kicks and the third goggles in surprise and then runs from the room. You sleep little for the rest of the night, gain 1 Endurance if you have lost any. In the morning you leave the city, on the road to Mortavalon. Turn to **254**.

226

As you spring towards Olvar he nods towards you and a lightning bolt stabs at you with a crack from the gem at his forehead. Your Defence against the lightning as you try to dodge is 6. If you dodge it turn to **406**. If you fail to dodge, turn to **85**.

227

The Cobra Man hisses, squirming on the end of his leash as the boy escapes to safety whilst the Cobra Man was distracted. The two men, hulking fat brutes who resemble the ox which pulls their wagon, tell you that they are taking the Cobra Man to the zoo in Mortavalon.

'We found him living alone in a cave not far up the hill there,' says one, pointing to a dark hole in the hillside overhung with rock. 'We didn't dare venture too far in but there's treasure to be had, I'll warrant.' With that, they whip the ox onwards, dragging the hissing Cobra Man behind them.

The boy sitting on the back of the wagon, calls, 'Thank you for saving me – don't shake hands with the young magician!' The men laugh and you are left to ponder the meaning of his strange words. Will you overtake the ox-cart and go straight to Mortavalon (turn to **283**) or enter the cave (turn to **275**)?

228

You drop to the ground in a slide and, before Yaemon knows what is happening, hook your legs around his, twist savagely and bring him toppling to the floor. Unable to use his legs, he is unable to break his fall adequately and he slams into the castle roof with a cry. He loses 2 Endurance. If this has killed Yaemon, turn to **420**. Otherwise he recovers quickly and, as you bring your knees up to your chest and snap your legs straight, flipping to land nimbly on your feet, he is on his feet ahead of you. But you still have the initiative. Will you try the Dragon's Tail throw again (turn to **245**), the Whirlpool throw (turn to **367**), a punch (turn to **266**) or a kick (turn to **390**)?

229

You unfurl the length of waxed string until it dangles just above the mouth of the Marshal of the Legion of Doom. You uncork the gourd which holds the blood of Nil, mouth of the Void, the most virulent poison known. It steams as the black beads run down the string and drop into Honoric's open mouth. He goes rigid and you know that he is helpless, dying of suffocation as his chest is paralyzed. You have assassinated the Marshal of the Legion of Doom, one of the most powerful men on Orb. Will you go down into the chamber and take the smoking sword, Sorcerak, (turn to **154**) or if you decide to leave without it will you cross the Keep roof to the turret which boasts the Black Whirlpool flag (turn to **130**) or the turret with the Scarlet Mantis flag (turn to **217**)?

230

As the wind whistles around the turrets of the Great Keep there is a sudden keening howl. For an instant the hairs on the back of your neck prickle with fear, until you realise that it is only the wind howling through an arrow slit in one of the turrets. The Captain looks startled and you choose this moment to pop up your head and blow a needle towards him through the swirling rain. He is lit only by the glow of the charcoal brazier, but the needle flies true to its target. He collapses to the floor with a clatter of armour as the wind howls again. You notice that each of the three turrets has an archway leading to a spiral staircase.

Which turret will you climb:

The turret flying the Sword of Doom flag? Turn to **320**.

The turret flying the Scarlet Mantis flag? Turn to **148**.

The turret flying the Black Whirlpool flag? Turn to **130**.

231

As the lions charge, you realise that even you are no match for them, nature's perfect killers. The crowd goes quiet. Are you an Acrobat? If you are, turn to **192**, if you are not, turn to **211**.

232

The ship which Glaivas has chartered, the 'Aquamarin' has a hundred oars and two masts. The winds are kind to you as you scud across the azure plain. The sea is so calm that after two weeks without the tang of salt spray on your lips you forget that it is composed of water at all. The oarsmen row for ten hours a day but they are free men, not chained to their oars. Two bear the scars of a pirate's persuader; captured by buccaneers, they are of the lucky few who have lived to see the sky again. All of them have the heavy upper body of the oarsman, some who turned to the sea for their livelihood too young are squat and mis-shapen, moulded by life at the oar into grotesque travesties of the mountain dwarves.

The Land of Plenty passes to the south and you are in sight of the Isle of the Magical Goddess when the lookout cries a warning. The helmsman steers a new course and the drum-beat quickens as the oarsmen redouble their efforts. The ship that is approaching is long and low, painted green and red and flying a red pennant at the top of its mast. Glaivas, standing next to you at the rail, says, 'That ship is from Port o' Reavers, we'll never outrun it.' So saying, he draws

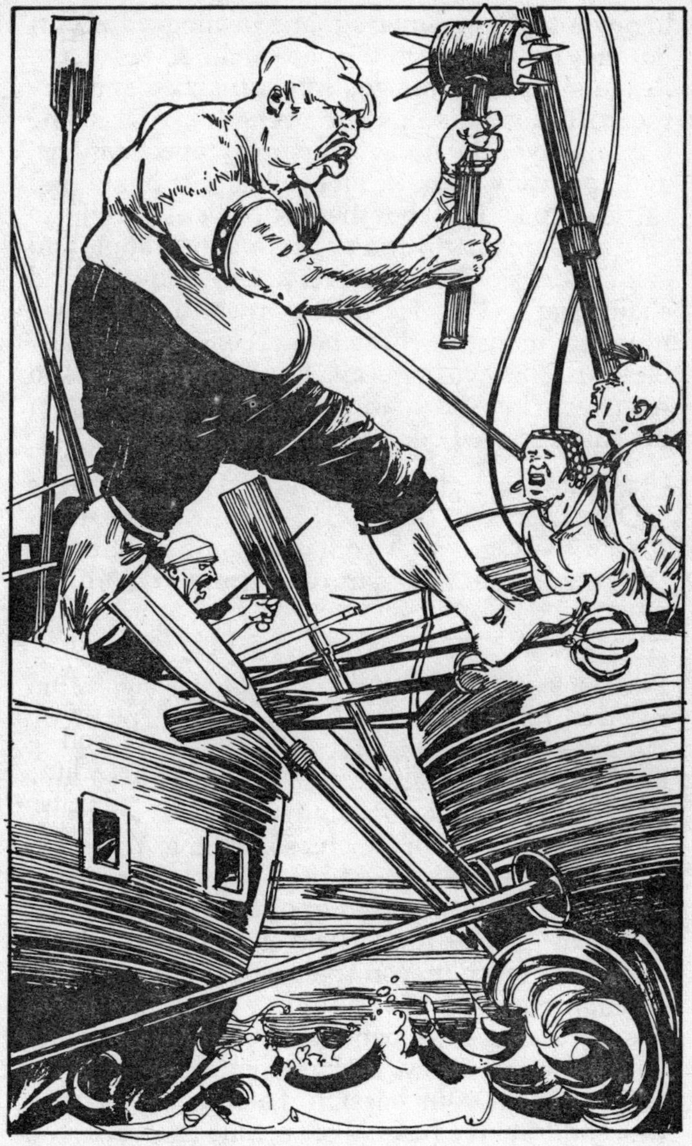

his sword. The oarsmen strain, sweating with effort but they cannot match the pace of the slaves on the Reavers' ship, galvanized into a frenzied spurt by the barbed whips of their overseers. At last the Captain gives the order 'prepare to repel boarders' and you ready yourself for combat. The pirate ship carries a spiked ram but they are obviously trying to take the Aquamarin as a prize for they grapple and come alongside. The Reavers carry scimitars and chain nets and are led in their rush to attack by a nine-foot monster whose body is covered in knobbles of mis-grown bone, an Ogre with a large spiked hammer. The Aquamarin's crew look no match for the battle-scarred buccaneers. Will you:

Leap into the rigging and hurl a Shuriken at the Ogre (turn to 257)?
Attack the Ogre as it comes aboard, flattening a section of the Aquamarin's rail (turn to 280)?

233

Runeweaver lies dead at your feet, his sword impaled in the wooden floor by his side. You pick it up but realise that he was indeed something of a magician as well as a warrior, for it needs a magician's spell to produce the pulsating spheres of green light which explode when they hit something. You reach for the Circlet but burn yourself when you touch it. Eldritch characters carved upon it show that it was forged deep in the Rift by dark elves. No-one of true heart may touch it. You spend the night in the hut and may regain up to 3 Endurance points. You leave the useless treasures behind; they would encumber you on your journey, and at daybreak you set out once more on your mission. Later in the day you descend from the heights of Fortune Pass. Will you head north east to the shores of the Sea of the Star and Druath Glennan (turn to **219**), due north towards the City of Far Snows (turn to **313**) or turn east through the Trollfens to Ionalbion and take ship across the Sea of the Star (turn to **59**)?

234

'Oh, but you are expected. Whimsical himself already knows of you, but not the Vile ones, it is not fated that they should know . . .' He pauses, '. . . yet.'

'Who is Whimsical?' you ask.

'The Theocrat of Fate, the ruler of Fiendil. You know so little stranger. Here is a golden touch for you, go to the Volunteer.' He points down the main street. 'You will hear something there to your advantage. Oh, we knew you were coming all right.' He breaks into a peal of laughter. Not wishing to draw further attention to yourself you hurry along the main street, Dreamer's Saunter. Fifty yards down the street hangs the sign of the Volunteer, a young warrior on bended knee receiving a sword from a man in golden robes, wearing a smiling golden mask. Will you take the old hermit's advice and go in (turn to **200**) or continue on down Dreamer's Saunter (turn to **185**)?

235

You gather grapes and nuts aplenty, living off the land, as you jog through the wilderness, checking your position by the position and height of the sun. You cover the ground quickly and are soon in a range of low hills crowned with cypress trees and, climbing up into one, you pass an untroubled and restful night. You may restore up to 2 Endurance. If

151

you wish to continue through the wilderness and pass north of Mortavalon, turn to **341**. If you wish to rejoin the road near the city to Mortavalon, turn to **212**.

236

The second monk hesitates slightly as you fling yourself into a feet-first slide at his legs. If this is the first time you have tried to throw him, his Defence against this surprising attack is only 5, not 6.

SECOND REVERENCER OF VILE
Defence against Dragon's Tail throw: 6
Endurance: 12
Damage: 1 Die

If you succeed, you hook your legs behind his and, twisting savagely, bring him to the ground. As he falls you pull your feet back and use your hands to raise your back off the ground, like a crab, and then flip up into an upright position. You may kick (turn to **264**) or punch your fallen attacker (turn to **244**) adding 1 to your Kick or Punch Modifier for this attack only.

If you failed to throw him, he leaps up above your sweeping throw, and lands on his feet, as you are springing up and tries to double-punch you with two successive strikes, your Defence is 7. If you are still alive you may kick (turn to **264**), or punch (turn to **244**).

237

You attempt to throw one of your assailants. He is sobering up but still quite drunk. His Defence against your Whirlpool throw is 5. If you throw him, turn to **296**. If you fail to throw him you will be attacked by whichever of your assailants is alive.

Your Defence against them is 7 if three are alive, 8 if two are alive, or 9 if only one remains alive. Each one will make an individual attack upon you and you may only block one of them. Each will do 1 Die + 1 Damage if they hit you. If you survive the attack, you may use the Winged Horse kick (turn to **256**) or the Iron Fist punch (turn to **248**).

238

As you strike with the side of your hand the Torturer blocks, his axe swinging by the thong from his wrist. He is a keen fist-fighter.

TORTURER
Defence against Tiger's Paw chop: 6
Endurance: 15
Damage: 1 Die

If you win turn to **224**. If the Torturer still lives he feints with the axe and tries a roundhouse punch with his other hand. Your Defence is 7. If you are still alive you may use the Leaping Tiger kick (turn to **249**), the Teeth of the Tiger Throw (turn to **259**) or you may try to punch again (return to the top of this paragraph).

239

As you spring towards Olvar, he nods at you and a lightning bolt stabs with a crack from the gem at his forehead. You try to leap above the lancing bolt. Your Defence against the bolt is 5. If you dodge it, turn to **165**. If you fail to dodge it, turn to **152**.

240

With incredible speed you spin to the right on the ball of your left foot, and whip your right heel around in an arc, as if your leg were a chain and your foot a heavy metal ball. It smashes into the side of Yaemon's face with a crack, spinning his head around, the force of the blow sends him whirling away, barely able to remain on his feet. Subtract 8 from his Endurance. Double this if you were using Inner Force. If he is dead turn to **420**. If he is still alive, you leap head-first towards him and somersault in the air, so that both your feet are hurtling towards him in a drop-kick. At the last instant he recovers and brings his right forearm across his face, sweeping your legs aside and down. You land nimbly, with your back to him, and acting quickly, whip your left foot up in an arc from left to right. This time Yaemon ducks and, as you turn to face him, you drive a Leaping Tiger kick at his face. Yaemon, under pressure, rears back, avoiding your foot by inches, and somersaults backwards onto his hands and then to his feet, repeating these flips until he is well out of range. You pursue him, and when he comes to a halt you are ready to attack again. Will you use Kwon's Flail again (turn to **54**), The Forked Lightning Strike kick (turn to **306**), The Winged Horse kick (turn to **84**), a punch (turn to **266**) or a throw (turn to **401**)?

241

You wait for Runeweaver to lunge at you, then sidestep to the right and try to grab his wrist, twist into him and throw him over your hip.

RUNEWEAVER
Defence against Whirlpool: 5
Endurance: 10
Damage: 1 Die + 2

If you throw him successfully, you may either punch (turn to **263**) or kick (turn to **250**) as he struggles to his feet, adding 2 to your Punch or Kick Modifier for this attack only.

If you fail to throw him, he pulls his sword arm back and aims a tremendous swipe at your head. Your Defence against his blade is 7.

If you survive, you may now punch (turn to **263**) or kick (turn to **250**).

242

He tells you that he is a monk who worships Kwon and invites you to go with him to his monastery in the Gardens of Redemption. The temple is set in a rose garden and you are happy to find a safe haven where you may meditate and seek help. You kneel at prayer in the bare temple and, beside you, the monk intones the psalm of Kwon the Redeemer. Turn to **221**.

243

As you step onto the plain the man in blue and gold moves onto the ice lake. The lions, slavering, rush towards you; they are large and strong. You cannot help admiring their speed and power. Will you meet them on the grass (turn to **231**) or retreat onto the ice lake (turn to **220**)?

244

The second monk comes to attack. Before he can kick, you dance forward and deliver a straight-fingered jab under his ribs.

SECOND REVERENCER OF VILE
Defence against Cobra Strike punch: 6
Endurance: 12
Damage: 1 Die

If you win, turn to **258**. If he is still alive he tries to throw you to the ground. Your Defence against the Mantis version of the Whirlpool throw is 7. If he throws you, you fly through the air, striking the ground, shoulder first; you roll to your feet, but the monk is ready for you and tries to kick. Your Defence against this is only 6 and you have no time to Block.

If you are still alive, you may use the Winged Horse (turn to **264**), the Dragon's Tail throw (turn to **326**), or the Cobra Strike again (return to the top of this paragraph).

245

You drop to the ground and try to catch his legs between yours and topple him over, but he is ready for you this time and leaps straight up and comes down on you, stamping on your midriff with a cry as he uses Inner Force. Your ribs crack like bamboo. Lose 10 Endurance, as he flips off you and spins in the air to land behind you facing your head. If you are still alive, you manage to overcome your pain and, looking up and to the rear, clap your hands together, with the speed and force of a bear trap around Yaemon's foot, as he tries to kick you again.

For a moment you think you have him, but he follows his kick through, pushing off with his other leg and, using your grip as a stepping stone, hurls himself the length of your body, pulling his leg from your grasp. You bring your knees up to your chest and snap your legs straight, using this momentum to flip to your feet, just in time to see Yaemon twisting in the air to land facing you once more. You have the initiative. Will you punch (turn to **266**), kick (turn to **390**) or try the Whirlpool throw (turn to **367**)?

246

You are immune to the toxic venom of the hooded cobra but not to the magicks which bound it within the Serpent Staff. Its jaw tightens inexorably in your neck and you tug wildly as its fangs near your jugular vein. In desperation, you rip its head from your neck, scattering its brains and gouging your own flesh horribly. Lose 4 Endurance. If you are still alive, you bandage your neck using a strip of lining from your costume and catch your breath before deciding which turret to enter next. Will it be the turret which flies the Sword of Doom banner if you have not done so already (turn to **339**) or that which boasts the Scarlet Mantis flag (turn to **370**)?

247

As the wind whistles around the turrets of the Great Keep there is a sudden keening howl. For an instant the hairs on the back of your neck prickle with fear, until you realise that it is nothing but the wind howling through an arrow-slit in one of the turrets. The Captain looks startled and you choose this moment to steal up behind him. He is alert and seems to sense you at the final moment. Make an Attack Roll as you lower the Garotte-wire over his head.

If you score 6–12: Turn to **178**.
If you score 2–5: Turn to **209**.

248

In the blink of an eye your fist flashes out at one of your attackers. You may choose which one.

	YOUNG CAPTAIN	1st SOLDIER	2nd SOLDIER
Defence against punch	4	4	4
Endurance	12	9	10
Damage	1 Die +3	1 Die +1	1 Die +1

If you have defeated them, turn to **268**. Each of the soldiers who is still alive will attack you individually. You cannot Block more than one and your Defence against each is 7 if three are alive, 8 if two are alive and 9 if only one remains alive. If you survive, will you use the Whirlpool throw (turn to **237**), the Winged Horse kick (turn to **256**) or punch again (return to the top of this paragraph)?

249

The Torturer is not used to an opponent who kicks

with such deadly power and breath-taking speed.

TORTURER
Defence against Leaping Tiger kick: 5
Endurance: 15
Damage: 1 Die + 1

If you win turn to **224**. If the Torturer still lives his axe thrums through the air as he tries to split your skull. Your Defence is 7. If you are still alive you may use the Tiger's Paw chop (turn to **238**), the Teeth of the Tiger throw (turn to **259**) or the Leaping Tiger kick once more (return to the top of this paragraph).

250

You step in to the right, and try to slam the top of your left foot into his midriff and then up to his throat in quick succession.

RUNEWEAVER
Defence against Forked Lightning Strike: 6
Endurance: 10
Damage: 1 Die + 1

If you have defeated him, turn to **233**. If he is still alive, he attacks you and your Defence against his chopping blow is 7.

If you are still alive, you may punch (turn to **263**), throw (turn to **241**) or kick again (return to the top of this paragraph).

251

Runeweaver makes a fire in the hut while you squat on the floor, to meditate. He wears only a breastplate of boiled leather for armour and you notice that he somehow starts the fire without a tinder box. Your spirit is wandering far away when the door to the hut is suddenly hurled open. A barbarian warrior strides in. He wears a necklace of giant weasel's teeth, a bearskin and a strange circlet with a deep blue gem at his forehead. His armour is curiously fashioned with overlapping plates, like a fish's scales. He points his longsword menacingly and demands in an uncouth norseman's bastardization of the common tongue, 'Well, my two small kobolds of the mountains, I'll take your money and all of your belongings.'

Runeweaver replies, 'What do you take us for, mere farmers or peasants that you should threaten us so?'

The Barbarian replies, 'I don't care if you're princes, I am Olvar the Chaos Bringer and I'm taking your gold'.

Will you:

Spring to the attack? Turn to **239**.
Hand him your money pouch? Turn to **216**.
Throw flash powder into the fire? Turn to **187**.

252

The ice is treacherous and only your fine sense of balance allows you to keep your footing as the Snow

161

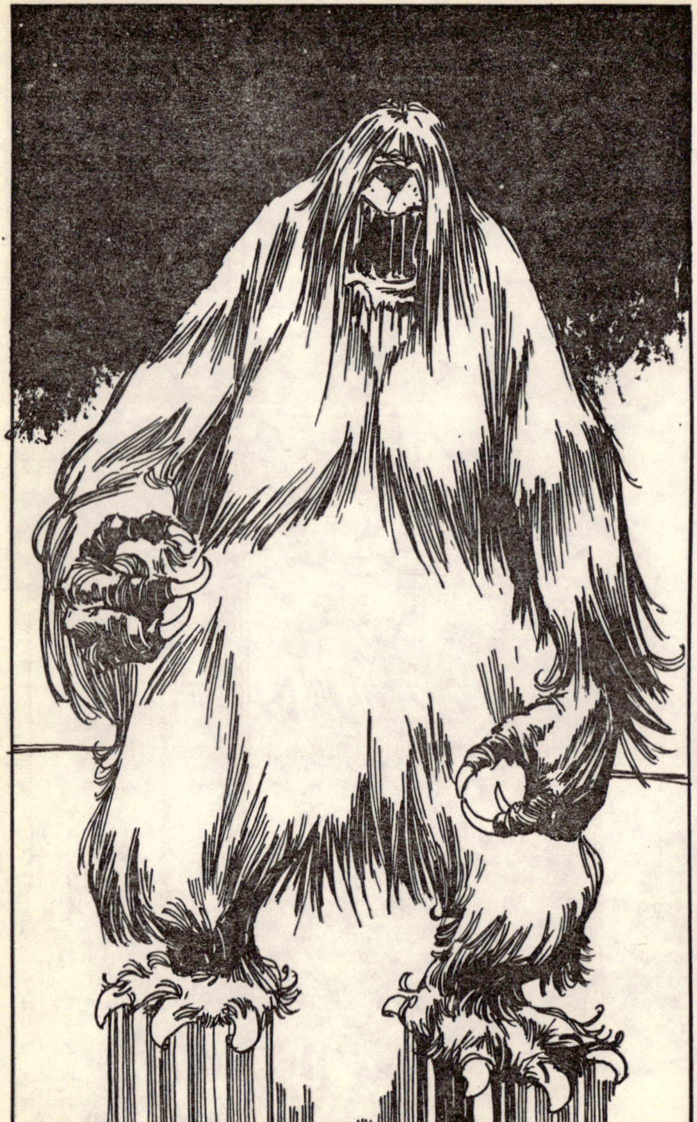

Giant bears down on you, waving its black talons. You cannot see its eyes but from its aggressive bearing you realise you must fight the white-furred colossus. Will you launch yourself into a slide across the ice and use the Dragon's Tail throw (turn to **202**), dart forward and use the Iron Fist punch (turn to **160**) or try the Forked Lightning Strike kick (turn to **184**)?

253

Your punch is so powerful that despite the magical field of force which protects him the magician folds and a Winged Horse kick sends him flying through the air into the moat. The water boils as the Floating Mouths latch onto their prey. Within a minute his flesh has been stripped to the bone. You climb up towards the Hobgoblin in his tower. The beast is showing off to the crowd, confident of another victory, beating his chest which is twice as broad as yours and twirling the trident in one hand. The tower is roughly built, with many hand-holds and you move around it, keeping the Hobgoblin confused as to your precise position. Then, holding an outcrop of stone with your hands you swing up into the tower behind him. He whirls round and you attack him with blinding speed. Will you use the Leaping Tiger kick (turn to **281**), the Whirlpool throw (turn to **267**) or the Tiger Paw chop (turn to **293**)?

254

As you leave the forbidding towered walls of Doomover behind, the sun climbs in the sky, ripening the corn and barley which rustles in the breeze. The fields do not stretch for far and you are soon on the edge of a low plain, the Plain of Feet, on which several thousand of the Legion of the Sword of Doom are practising for the forthcoming war, smart and efficient. The smooth plain gradually gives way to a wilderness of trees and vines. Will you continue along the road to Mortavalon (turn to **223**) or strike north of the road, into the wilderness (turn to **235**)?

255

The man turns aside, as if he had made a mistake, and you make your way out of the press of bodies as quickly as you can. You have become well known in Mortavalon, your exploits in the arena are on everyone's lips and you decide that it is prudent to leave this city, with its pre-occupation with violent death. You leave by the northern arch, disguised as someone who works the land. The gateguards ask you where you are going, 'It is the day of the games, a holiday,' but you ignore them and they let you go. Will you strike north-east across the wastelands to the city of Fiendil (turn to **260**) or head due north to Storm Giant's Causeway, in the Mountains of Vision (turn to **81**)?

256

You step forward onto your right foot then bring your left foot up, spin to the right and lash your left heel high into the air, at one of your attackers' heads. You may choose which one.

	YOUNG CAPTAIN	1st SOLDIER	2nd SOLDIER
Defence against kick	5	4	4
Endurance	12	9	10
Damage	1 Die +3	1 Die +1	1 Die +1

If you have defeated them, turn to **268**. Each of the soldiers will attack you individually. You cannot block more than one and your Defence against each is 7 if three are alive, 8 if two are alive and 9 if only one still lives. If you survive, will you use the Whirlpool throw (turn to **237**), the Iron Fist punch (turn to **248**) or kick again (return to the top of this paragraph)?

257

Your Shuriken glints in the sun as it hurtles towards its mark in the Ogre's chest. As you leap down from the rigging a volley of arrows is let loose from the stern castle of the Reaver's ship. The Ogre grunts with pain as the Shuriken lodges in its chest. Throw one Die and take the score from the huge beast's Endurance of 16. One of the pirate's arrows is coming at you. Do you have the skill of Arrow Cutting? If you have turn to **380**. If you have not, turn to **396**.

258

The second monk is barely conscious but he kneels before you in the street, submitting to your superior power and ability. Will you spare him (turn to **409**) or finish him off with a kick to the head (turn to **222**)?

259

The Torturer is taken by surprise at your amazing leap, he almost drops the axe which swings by its thong from his wrist as he tries to throw your leg back from his head.

TORTURER
Defence against Teeth of the Tiger throw: 6
Endurance: 15
Damage: 1 Die + 1

If you throw him successfully you may follow up with a Leaping Tiger kick (turn to **249**) or a Tiger's Paw chop (turn to **238**) while he is down, adding 2 to your Punch or Kick Modifier for this attack only. If you fail to throw him, he catches your feet and hurls you back against the wall of the torture chamber, lose 2 Endurance. If you are still alive he then follows up with his swinging axe. Your Defence as you roll aside is 7. If you are still alive you spring to your feet. You may now kick (turn to **249**) or punch (turn to **238**).

260

The journey across the waste lands takes four days. If you have been hurt you may restore up to 6 points of Endurance. For much of the way you follow the banks of the river of Fortune which is joined by a little-trodden track stretching from Fiendil to Greyguilds-on-the-Moor, the City of Learning far to the south. It rains on the third day and for the first time you notice that the climate is much cooler than that of the islands in the Endless Sea. At last, as the mountains loom ahead, you see the city of Fiendil in a verdant valley. The city walls are ill-kempt, in places even breached, and there are no guards at the gate, only an old man in a wine-stained toga, sitting on a stone block which was once part of the battlements of the gate-tower. You are about to pass him by when he calls softly to you, 'Avenger, well-met in Fiendil, you have travelled far from the Island of Tranquil Dreams.' He is weak with age and seems to hold no threat for you, save that somehow he knows who you are. There is no-one else in sight. Do you implore him to say nothing about you to anyone (turn to **234**) or kill him with a deft chop to the head (turn to **114**)?

261

The floor of the arena is divided into sections. In the centre a huge Hobgoblin, brandishing a trident, stands at the top of a miniature castle, which is surrounded by a large moat. The circle outside the moat is divided into four sectors by fences of iron spikes. The sector to your left is a small plain of grass, to your right is a frozen lake, created magically. Beyond the plain is a lurid green swamp and between swamp and ice is a desert of sand dunes. You are standing on a platform between the grass and ice.

At the opposite side of the arena a man in silver armour, his face hidden by his visor, stands on a similar platform. Between you both, to your left is a Dark Elf, waving her blacksteel sword defiantly and at the edge of the arena to your right stands a young man in flowing blue and gold robes. On the ice-lake stands a Snow Giant, ten feet tall, two roaring lions roam the plain. You can see nothing but a boat in the swamp and in the desert waits a man with the swaying head and neck of a cobra. As you look around you the platform begins to slide down towards the ground and you will soon be within reach of the lions or the Snow Giant. Indeed, they can now move freely into each other's area. The walls of the arena are sheer and lined with the spears of soldiers. The man in armour steps onto the dunes as the Dark Elf wades into the swamp. The man in the blue and gold robes waits, still. Will you move to the plain and take your chances with the lions (turn to **243**) or step onto the ice lake (turn to **252**)?

PLAN OF THE ARENA IN MORTAVALON

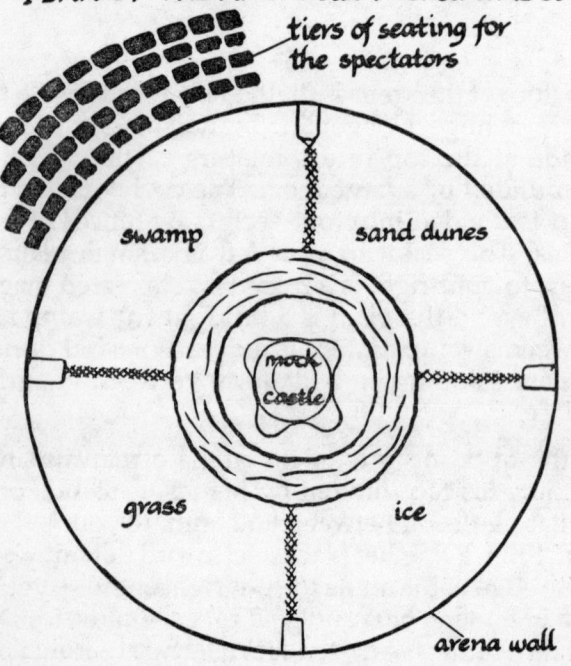

tiers of seating for the spectators

swamp *sand dunes*

mock castle

grass *ice*

arena wall

⎕ *descending platform*
✕ *fence of spikes*
≡ *moat*

262

You make a small fire in the hut before squatting on the floor to meditate. Your spirit is wandering far away when the door to the hut is suddenly hurled open. A barbarian warrior strides in. He wears a necklace of giant weasel's teeth, a bearskin and a strange circlet with a deep blue gem at his forehead. His armour is curiously fashioned with overlapping plates, like a fish's scales. He points his longsword menacingly and demands in an uncouth norseman's bastardization of the common tongue, 'Well, my small kobold of the mountains, Olvar the Chaos Bringer is going to take all of your money!' Will you:

Spring to the attack? Turn to **226**.
Hand him your money pouch? Turn to **204**.
Throw flash powder into the fire? Turn to **117**.

263

You chop with the speed of a striking snake towards the side of Runeweaver's neck.

RUNEWEAVER
Defence against Tiger's Paw: 5
Endurance: 10
Damage: 1 Die + 1

If you have defeated him, turn to **233**. If he is still alive, he sweeps his sword at your legs. Your Defence is 6 as you try to leap above the blade.

If you survive, you may kick (turn to **250**), throw (turn to **241**) or punch again (return to the top of this paragraph).

264

The second monk comes to attack. You turn sideways on and unleash a Winged Horse kick as he approaches.

SECOND REVERENCER OF VILE
Defence against Winged Horse kick: 7
Endurance: 12
Damage: 1 Die

If you win, turn to **258**. If he is still alive he answers you kick for kick, your Defence is 8. If you are still alive, you may use the Cobra Strike punch (turn to **244**), the Dragon's Tail throw (turn to **236**) or kick again (return to top of this paragraph).

265

You jump up and swing from the hole which leads to the attic, then squeeze through onto the planks beyond. Testing for loose boards, you crawl carefully to a crack in the ceiling. A single candle burning in the chamber below gives just enough light to see by. Honoric is asleep, his arrogant features seem less cruel than in his waking hours and his mouth is open as he snores gently. His great sword lies unsheathed beside him. You cannot spot any traps in the chamber. If you would like to pour your single dose of Blood of Nil poison down a waxed string into Honoric's mouth turn to **229**. If you prefer to get back down to the staircase and go in through the door after oiling its hinges turn to **274**.

266

Which punch will you try?

The Cobra Strike? Turn to **340**.
The Iron Fist? Turn to **330**.
The Tiger's Paw? Turn to **410**.

You must decide now if you wish to use Inner Force.

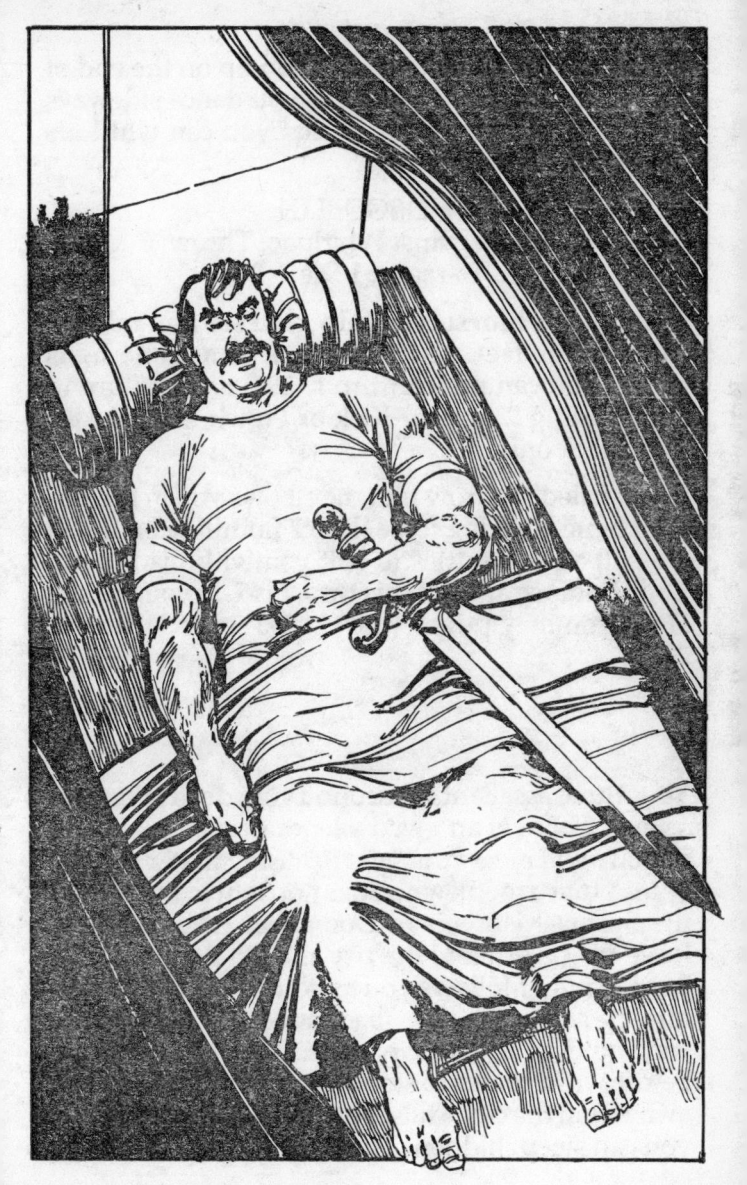

171

267

The Hobgoblin tries to shovel you up on the end of his wickedly barbed trident as you dance sideways and try to grab its shaft so that you can whirl his heavy body over your hip.

HOBGOBLIN
Defence against Whirlpool Throw: 6
Damage: 1 Die + 3

If you throw him successfully, you see him roll and come to his feet, but you attack him while he is rising. You can punch (turn to **293**) or kick (turn to **281**), adding 2 to your Kick or Punch Modifier for that attack only.

If you failed to throw him, he elbows you in the ribs with bone cracking force (lose 2 Endurance). If you are still alive, he tries to spit you with his trident. Your Defence against this thrust is 7. If you are still alive, you may punch (turn to **293**) or kick (turn to **281**).

268

Your three assailants lie around you, dead or unconscious. There is an awed silence in the tavern and nobody will meet your eye. Realising that word will spread that a monk who does not fight in the style of the Scarlet Mantis is in Doomover, you decide to leave the tavern and the city as soon as possible. A young soldier follows you as you leave but you give him the slip in a maze of back streets and make your way quickly to the city gate. You pass through before word comes to stop all strangers. Once safely away from the city walls, you climb into a tree where you can sleep, hidden. Turn to **254**.

269

Leaping onto the flat roof of the Great Keep you send a throwing star whistling towards the Captain's head. Make an Attack roll.

If you score 9–12: Turn to **189**.
If you score 6–8: Turn to **199**.
If you score 2–5: Turn to **218**.

270

A steep stairway winds up from the torture chamber, past empty cells. You emerge into a hallway within the Great Keep itself. A spiral stairway winds upwards from the opposite side of the stone hallway. If you have the skill of Picking Locks, turn to **215**. If you do not have this skill, turn to **207**.

271

You leap out and into the air, grabbing one of the Arocs as it swoops behind the warrior. With a powerful wrench you break its neck. A sharp talon tears your shoulder (lose 3 Endurance), if you are still alive you turn and grab your attacker's leg, pulling him down and then delivering a crippling Tiger's Paw to the side of its neck as another magical bolt leaps from the warrior's sword. Seeing this, the

Arocs glide out across the valley, leaving you to continue on your way. The warrior introduces himself as Runeweaver. You know that runes are the symbols used in spell making. He thanks you for aiding him and tells you he is a wandering adventurer who is travelling north to find pastures new, after a somewhat embarrassing brush with the authorities at Mortavalon. You walk together for a while until you come to a small hut, near the source of the river. You decide to pass the night there – Runeweaver hopes to light a fire against the cold. Turn to **251**.

272

The crowd cheer as you throw the Hobgoblin's trident into the moat, and the castle itself begins to sink into the ground. Searching the vile body of the swart beast you find a phial marked 'Magic Potion'; the Hobgoblin's prize for winning in the arena, it had been his most prized possession. Removing the stopper, you detect the unmistakable odour of Essence of Firenewt, not a magic potion at all. The Hobgoblin had been tricked, but you may find a use for it and decide to keep it. The castle disappears from the view of the ecstatic populace of Mortavalon, whose blood-lust you have temporarily sated, and a passage leads you to the street outside. A press of people gathers round you. An aristocrat's butler offers you a job as a bodyguard as you are both showered with rose-blooms. You try to get away from these unwanted attentions but a man tugs at your iron sleeve. You turn, ready to Cobra Strike, but he says, 'Do you come from the Island of Tranquil Dreams?' Do you admit that you do (turn to **242**) or say that you have never heard of such an island (turn to **255**)?

273

As you pass by the tavern, its door swings open and raucous noise and the reek of stale sweat from within greets you. You walk on by and casually examine the monastery. Beautiful towers and arches adorn it. Its cloisters are well-guarded and the edges of its roof are barbed with spikes. Behind it is a refectory and sleeping quarters. You decide to use your skills as a Ninja to gain entry at night and hunt for information. Is Yaemon somewhere within? Will you reconnoitre the monastery to find the safest way of entry (turn to 323) or spend the day in a hostel practising the Way of the Tiger (turn to 303)?

274

The door swings open easily on its oiled hinges and you glide silently into the chamber. You feel the shadow of fear which comes from Honoric's sword, Sorcerak which suddenly speaks his name. Amazingly, he is awake immediately, rolling off the far side of the bed as he clutches the talking sword. You hurdle the bed but he is ready for you and he shouts out loud as a battle royal begins. He grunts with pain as you lash your foot into his side, but he is a hard man and his skill with the sword is breathtaking. He shears clean through your sleeve irons and your left arm is broken and useless but you reply with a great punch which knocks him backwards. Fear shows on Honoric's face as he comprehends your deadliness, but he attacks with new ferocity. Without warning you are felled by a blow from behind and, looking up, you see Yaemon's impassive face as Honoric's blade pierces your heart, ending your life.

275

The cave is dark, but light filters down into it from a

narrow crack in the ceiling. As you inch your way along the uneven floor you hear footsteps behind you and hurry on into the darkness. Steps lead down and, as you descend, a curious noise like the grinding of metal cogs sounds above. Suddenly a torrent of water cascades down the steps and you run on through the darkness, feeling the wall with your hand. You are soon knee-deep and beginning to wonder if there is any way out at the end of the tunnel when a portcullis slams to the floor behind you. The level of water drops and you find yourself trapped in an iron cage. There is no escape and you languish in the cage for some hours, using the time to relax and meditate. Suddenly the cage is flooded with light as a door at the end of the tunnel is flung open. You are under the seats of a huge circular arena which is slowly filling with people. The huge crowd cheers as a trumpet sounds and the front of the cage collapses to the ground. A group of soldiers come to the back of the cage and motion you to step out into the arena, poking spears through the portcullis.

'May Fate smile on you,' says one. 'Only one of you can become the king of the castle, and live.'

You step out into the sunlight to another cheer from the crowd, and the cage front is pulled up again behind you and you cannot go back. Squinting in the sun you look around you. Turn to **261**.

276

The warrior-magician hefts his sword normally now, poised to thrust or parry. Perhaps there is no magic left in his sword, you wonder as you decide whether to use the Forked Lightning Strike (turn to

250), the Whirlpool throw (turn to **241**) or the Tiger's Paw chop (turn to **263**).

277

You fit yourself into the hole which passes through the ten foot thick wall just before another soldier passes by on his round of the inner courtyard. Mercifully he doesn't notice your black-garbed form in the darkness of the hole. You lie still for half an hour until you have timed how long his round takes, and then try to move on, only to find you have become wedged, but dislocating your shoulder allows you to squeeze through. You dart to the Great Keep and begin the climb to its roof, hanging motionless by the Cat's Claws each time the guard's beat takes him below you. If you wish to continue outside the Keep until you reach the roof turn to **174**. If you want to force entry at one of the lower windows turn to **2**.

278

You lash the ball of your right foot straight at Yaemon's stomach, but he hops back on both feet and catches your foot. He heaves upwards and you are sent into the air; but you use this throw to your advantage, and whip your left foot up into his face as you somersault backwards through the air. He cries in pain. Subtract 2 from his Endurance. If Yaemon is killed, turn to **420**. If he is still alive he is enraged and just as you land nimbly on your feet he is up beside you. He twists to the side and whips the top of his right foot into your solar plexus, then up to your face and down to your ribcage again, in quick succession, with three clipped shouts. Lose 8 Endurance. If you are still alive, his last blow hurls you flat on your back. As your head clears, you look up to see Yaemon above you, legs astride your torso, his fist driving down at your face. Desperately, you slap it aside with your right hand, and bring it back across your chest to deflect another vicious chop to your neck. It takes only a split second to snake your left hand around his leg and heave, bringing him down to the ground. Quickly you disengage and spring to your feet, as does Yaemon. He is moments behind you, and you may launch an attack. Will you use the Winged Horse kick (turn to **84**), the Forked Lightning Strike kick (turn to **306**), Kwon's Flail kick, if you have been taught it (turn to **240**), a punch (turn to **266**) or a throw (turn to **401**)?

279
The monk falls to the ground, helplessly coughing blood, but there is no respite for you, as the second monk bows to you before preparing to attack. You decide to change your tactics. Will you use the Dragon's Tail throw (turn to **236**), the Cobra Strike jab (turn to **244**) or the Winged Horse kick (turn to **264**)?

280
The Ogre tramples the wooden rail, and raises its hammer to smash you as you land nimbly before it. A volley of arrows from the pirate ship's stern-castle whistles above you. Do you:

Try to deliver a Winged Horse kick (turn to **332**)?
Attempt the Iron Fist punch (turn to **310**)?
Slide across the deck and use the Dragon's Tail throw (turn to **345**)?

281
The Hobgoblin tries to transfix you with his wick-

edly barbed trident as you jump into the air and lash out with the ball of your foot, hoping to take him in the throat.

HOBGOBLIN
Defence against Leaping Tiger kick: 6
Endurance: 18
Damage: 1 Die + 3

If you kill the Hobgoblin, turn to **272**. If the Hobgoblin is still alive, he jabs the trident at your stomach. Your Defence against this jab as you dodge in the confined space atop the turret, is 8. If you are still alive after his attack, you may try a Tiger's Paw punch (turn to **293**), the Whirlpool throw (turn to **267**) or the Leaping Tiger again (return to the top of this paragraph).

282

In the wink of an eye you have buried a throwing star in the Torturer's back and disappeared below the inky black water. Staring out from beneath the surface, you see the Torturer turn in pain and then threaten the boy with the red hot iron and the boy points to the water. The enraged Torturer turns his hooded face towards the water and, seizing his axe, runs screaming to the pool. You erupt from the water and unleash another Shuriken, which takes him in the arm before he hits the surface. As he gasps in pain, you use the Tiger's Paw to knock the axe from his grasp and wrestle with him as you sink into the black depths. He is strong but no match for you underwater. You have trained for this and use repeated Cobra Strikes to pummel him into helplessness, the water barely lessening the speed of your blows. The Torturer floats lifeless to the surface and you drag yourself, gasping, into the torture chamber. There are several prisoners and they implore you to release them and, seizing the opportunity to create a diversion, you do so, asking only that they wait to the count of two hundred before following you out of the chamber. Turn to **270**.

283

The road winds down from the hills and you see the city of Mortavalon, nestling in a bowl of green pastures and cornfields. The entrance to the city is through a large triumphal arch dedicated to a victory won by the Empire hunters who follow the god of Empire, Moraine, against the Soldiers of Fate. It is evening and you fall in with a group of peasants who have been working the land. Explaining that you are a stranger you ask them about their city. It seems that the largest temple is to the god, Death, but the priests seldom interfere in daily life, as long as no-one quibbles over the occasional disappearance. They practise child-sacrifice. Tomorrow is to be a holiday for there is a combat in the arena. It seems they are looking for a champion who may win a fabulous fortune. If you would like to follow one of them to visit the Master of the Arena, turn to **290**. If you would rather walk on through the city turn to **169**.

284

The warrior fights well but after a time no more magical bolts flare forth from his sword and he is tumbled off the path. The bird-men kill him and carry him off to their ledges. You go on your way and eventually reach a hut near the source of the river. The cold does not affect you long as you are moving, as you trained long and hard to withstand extremes of climate, but you decide to spend the night inside as you will be safe from the bird-men. Turn to **262**.

285

You try to somersault over the guards but you are too slow and one of them slashes you with his sword as you pass overhead. You fall to the ground and before you can get up one of them plunges his sword into your back, forcing you down to the muddy road. He has ruptured your liver and you die. Your adventure ends here.

286

As the two monks close in to kick at you, you launch yourself feet first at the head of one. If this is the first time you have attempted this move, they are taken by surprise. The number after the slash under Defence against Throw refers to their Defence if this is the second (or third etc) time that you have tried this. You may choose only one to attack.

	1st Monk	2nd Monk
Defence against Teeth of the Tiger Throw	5/6	5/6
Endurance	14	13
Damage	1 Die + 1	1 Die + 1

If you succeed in throwing one, you may follow up with a punch (turn to **353**) or a kick (turn to **374**), adding 1 to your Punch or Kick Modifier for this attack only.

If you have failed to throw him, you find yourself at

a disadvantage as you land and your Defence against them is 5 if two remain alive (and you can only block one of their attacks) and 7 if there is only one left. If you survive you may use the Winged Horse kick (turn to 374), or the Tiger's Paw chop (turn to 353).

287
You fall backwards from the Hall of Webs, onto the flagstones of the courtyard below, breaking your neck. You have failed.

288
You leap high into the air and somersault towards Runeweaver, over the speeding bolt which explodes against the wall of the hut with a bang. Turn to 276.

289
There is no one at the north gate to see you leave the strange city of Fiendil, but you decide to put as much distance between yourself and its inhabitants as quickly as you can. Are you wearing an Opal Ring? If you are, turn to 203. If you are not, turn to 213.

290
The peasant who has been leading you stops outside a grand white building and points inside. You thank him and enter the cool marble-floored building, striding confidently towards a warrior dressed in a blue and gold toga. Suddenly the floor opens up

underneath you and you are pitched downwards to the floor of a dark tunnel below. The man in the toga shouts down after you, 'Hurry friend, to the arena. If my men catch you first they will kill you.' You can see no way out save down the tunnel ahead of you. Turn to 275.

291

The brazier splutters in the wash of water that sprays the chamber as you leap behind the Torturer. He blindly whips the red-hot iron round behind him and is lucky to catch you with it. You lose 2 Endurance as it bites agonisingly into your flesh. If you are still alive, you spring back from the iron as he lets it fall and pulls the axe from his belt. He grins murderously at you. Will you wipe the grin from his face with a Leaping Tiger kick (turn to 249), a Tiger's Paw chop (turn to 238) or the Teeth of the Tiger throw (turn to 259)?

292

The star flies into the bolt and spins away with a whine. The bolt is thrown off course and explodes harmlessly with a bang. You circle Runeweaver, looking for an opening. Turn to 276.

293

As the Hobgoblin whirls the butt of the trident towards your side, you chop the side of your hand down into his warty shoulder.

HOBGOBLIN
Defence against Tiger's Paw: 5
Endurance: 18
Damage: 1 Die + 1

If you kill the Hobgoblin, turn to 272. If the Hobgoblin is still alive, you must try to leap over the flailing butt of his trident. Your Defence against this great sweep is 8. If you are still alive, you may use the Leaping Tiger kick (turn to **281**), the Whirlpool throw (turn to **267**) or use the Tiger's Paw again (return to the top of this paragraph).

294

The seaweed cracks underfoot as you approach the city of Ionalbion, perched on white cliffs above the Sea of the Star. Flocks of sheep flee from you as you climb the rolling downlands outside the land gate. The guards bear a token you do not recognise, a dancing sword with a scroll wrapped around its blade. The street stretches towards the sea gate and the harbour. You pass a fountain in the shape of a dolphin where a young woman sells flowers made of coloured marzipan outside one of the many scroll shops. Guessing that most travellers would pass by the fountain you ask her if she has noticed anyone unusual in the past tenday. She replies in a guttural version of the common-tongue that, although she sits by the fountain every day, she has seen no one unusual. You decide to go straight to the harbour, where a number of long low-sided biremes are tied up. A placard advertises that 'the Porpoise' sails for Druath Glennan at high tide. The fare is two pieces of gold. You board the ship as they are about to cast off, paying the gold to a cabin boy. Turn to **337**.

295

You grab the Two-headed Giant around the thighs, but it weighs well over a ton and you find yourself unable to throw it. The monster drops its colossal club and grabs you, throwing you to the rock under foot and trampling you. Your head splits like a ripe melon as the force of its heel grinds downwards. You have failed your mission.

296

You manage to dodge underneath the sword cut of one of the soldiers, grab his arm, twist, and whirl him round your hip. You bring him down onto a small table with a splintering crash. Someone comments on your unusual fighting style. You hurdle the heap of broken bones and wood and are out of the tavern before anyone else can move against you. You are not followed and decide to sleep in a hostel for the night at a cost of one gold piece. In the morning, you decide to set off north, lest Yaemon reach the Pillars of Change before you, and leave the city on the road to Mortavalon. Turn to **254**.

297

You tell the priest of your quest to stop Yaemon causing the imprisonment of your god, Kwon, in Inferno. His brow is furrowed as he says, 'I would not be so worried if it were not for the fact that Yaemon's monks of the Scarlet Mantis are in league with the accursed Legion of the Sword of Doom.' He goes on to say that Honoric, Marshal of the Legion, has left Doomover just when his men were expecting him to lead them in battle against the people of the Spires of Foreshadowing. He left with Yaemon and they rode alone, towards Mortavalon.

'Surely you don't think that you alone can stop them. Honoric slew forty men, battle-hardened veterans, at the battle of the Hollow Tower. Three Tools of Fate died beneath his Eldritch blade, Sorcerak, that day. You have no weapons. No man can stand against Yaemon in unarmed combat, he has been Grandmaster for a hundred seasons.'

'What you say may be true, but I have sworn to try.'

He can tell you no more but he gives you a small flask containing a clear blue liquid. It is a Potion of Healing and you may use it once, at any time when you are not in combat, to restore up to ten lost Endurance points. You thank the priest and, intent on catching up with Yaemon, leave the temple. Will you:

Leave the city by the harbour gate and head for Mortavalon (turn to 65)?
Go through the Obsidian Gate into Doomover (turn to 6)?

298

You manage to grab the rope in mid air and slow your fall, dropping the last five yards and landing on your feet when the monk dislodges the grappling hook. You sweep it up and disappear into the city before he can give the alarm. You lie low until morning and leave the city, disguised once more as a beggar, intent on making sure that Yaemon doesn't reach the Pillars of Change before you. Turn to 254.

299

The Toy-maker screams wretchedly behind you as you pass quickly by. Keeping away from monks you spend some time walking the otherwise quiet streets of this city that seems almost out of touch with the rest of the Manmarch. You find out nothing, no one seems to care enough even to speak more than a few pleasantries to you. In despair you decide to head north once more. You have no way of knowing whether Yaemon is still ahead of you but you cannot risk allowing him to reach the Pillars of Change before you. Turn to **289**.

300

The roof of the shack leaks and the smell of damp is everywhere but the old woman who lives there with her imbecile son asks no questions and feeds you some hot gruel. You thank her and leave two pieces of gold beneath a jar in the pantry, where she will later come across them, before settling down to wait. It is after dusk when there is a fluttering outside the cobweb strewn window. You throw it open and Deirdra's white dove flies in, dropping a piece of paper from its beak into your lap before fluttering away over the city walls. The note reads:

> Make all haste to Quench-heart Keep. Your quarry has left the monastery of Vile within the city to stay at the Keep before crossing the snows to the Pillars of Change.

You ask the woman the way but she grows terrified at the mention of the castle, imploring you not to go there. 'I must,' you insist and at length she directs you to walk north west across the Wold, towards the Goblin Teeth Mountains. You skirt the city and strike out across country at a sign which advertises a tavern called the Hydra's Heads. Turn to **179**.

301

You step to the right and, with your legs apart and your knees bent slightly, cleave the air with your left

187

arm driving from your hip in towards Yaemon's throat. Ready for you this time, he reacts with lightning reflexes. He leans back and whips the palm of his left hand up and across. He slams into the inside of your wrist whilst his right hand slams into your left tricep, just above your elbow. The pain is excruciating as your arm is forced against its joint and snaps with a crack. Lose 8 Endurance. If you are still alive, you may not punch again, nor will you be able to use Acrobatics if you have this skill. As you stagger backwards in agony, you desperately try to overcome the pain in time to deal with Yaemon's next attack. You look up to see him leaping through the air towards you, his left leg extended in a Flying Winged Horse kick aimed at your head. You have no choice but to try and block it. Your Defence is 7. If you succeed, turn to **411**. If you fail, turn to **24**.

302

The Barbarian's voice rises to a shriek of battle lust as he swipes at you, berserk. He cares nothing for your attacks so long as his sword tastes your blood. Subtract one from any damage you do to him. He cuts his sword down towards your head, but you sidestep to the right, twist and lash your foot towards his face as his sword whistles down past your back.

OLVAR THE BARBARIAN
Defence against Winged Horse: 7
Endurance: 18
Damage: 1 Die + 1

If you have defeated Olvar, turn to **344**. If he still lives, he swings his sword from right to left through the point where you are standing. Your Defence is 8 as you hop backwards.

If you are still alive you may punch (turn to **377**), throw (turn to **318**) or kick again (return to the top of this paragraph).

303

It is well after midnight when you emerge from the hostel into the cool night air, dressed in your black costume and hood. Approaching the monastery, you can see that the climb to the roof of the hallway which connects the refectory to the hall of worship is an easy one because barrels of wine have been stacked against the wall. You gain the roof and descend into a very small courtyard. Turning a corner of the courtyard wall, you are faced with a dead end. The only way out which you can see is a small passageway leading off to the left. You edge carefully down it but snap an unseen thread, as thin as spiderweave, which sets a bell jingling in the refectory. You run on down the passageway which turns left again only to find another dead end from which there is no escape. The passages are specially designed to lead an intruder to an inescapable hole and that is where you now find yourself. Several monks appear behind you and you frantically try to climb the wall, only to find that it is coated with a slimy web to which you stick fast. You are helpless and can only kill yourself before they take you, by biting off your own tongue so that you bleed to death. Your adventure ends here.

304

Togawa nods again and asks a third question, 'What are your eyes?'

'My eyes are the Sun and the Moon,' you say, reciting the words from the secret Litany of the Ninja Grandmasters. 'I am Ninja, I follow the Way of the Tiger.'

Togawa beams at you, 'A Grandmaster of the Five Winds,' he says, 'I must do my best to help you.' You sleep on the cold floor of the cave, but in your dreams, Togawa, his body silver and ethereal, appears to you, stretching out his hand. You take it and he lifts you out of your body. Looking down, you can see yourself, asleep, in the candlelight. Soon, you are far from the cave, washed by ethereal wind. You hold on tight, knowing that without Togawa's guidance, you would drift helplessly; the skills of the Ninja cannot aid you here. The monk points ahead to a gleaming archway beyond which a silver pathway stretches up into the clouds. Cherubs flock around its pillars and a Guardian Angel, flawless and white, stands between them.

'This is the Gateway to the Seven Heavens,' says Togawa. 'We may not enter yet.' As he speaks, a sinuous form takes shape on the silver road. It glides past the Guardian Angel and as it approaches, you see that it is a perfect tiger, but its fur is white and its eyes are blue.

'The Spirit Tiger is a servant of Kwon,' says Togawa. 'She will help us.' As the tigress looks at you, she passes on a part of her knowledge. She has stalked Yaemon, on the Ethereal Plane, undetected, even by him. Yaemon and Honoric, Marshal of the Legion of the Sword of Doom who worships the god, Vasch-Ro, are journeying to the far-away city of Druath Glennan at the edge of the Far Snows. They will meet a third there, Manse the Deathmage, a potent and evil sorcerer, who reverences Nemesis, the Supreme Principle of Evil. Together they plan to journey to the Pillars of Change and each knows a secret word which will bind a god or goddess in Inferno. You realise that you must journey to Druath Glennan as quickly as possible. The Spirit Tiger blesses you and Fate will smile on you. Your Fate Modifier is now + 1. You try to speak to the Spirit Tiger but words will not come and Togawa pulls you away from the Gateway to the Seven Heavens.

When you awake in the morning he says, 'The unholy alliance must be stopped. Of all the evil gods, only the followers of Vile, Vasch-Ro and Nemesis would have the discipline to join together. Nemesis is the greatest of the evil gods. Never before have three such powerful and evil men trusted each other.' He pulls a bag of herbs from a crack in the rock. 'These have healing virtue,' he says. You take them and may use them at any time when you are not being attacked to restore up to 8 Endurance. You thank him and are about to ask him

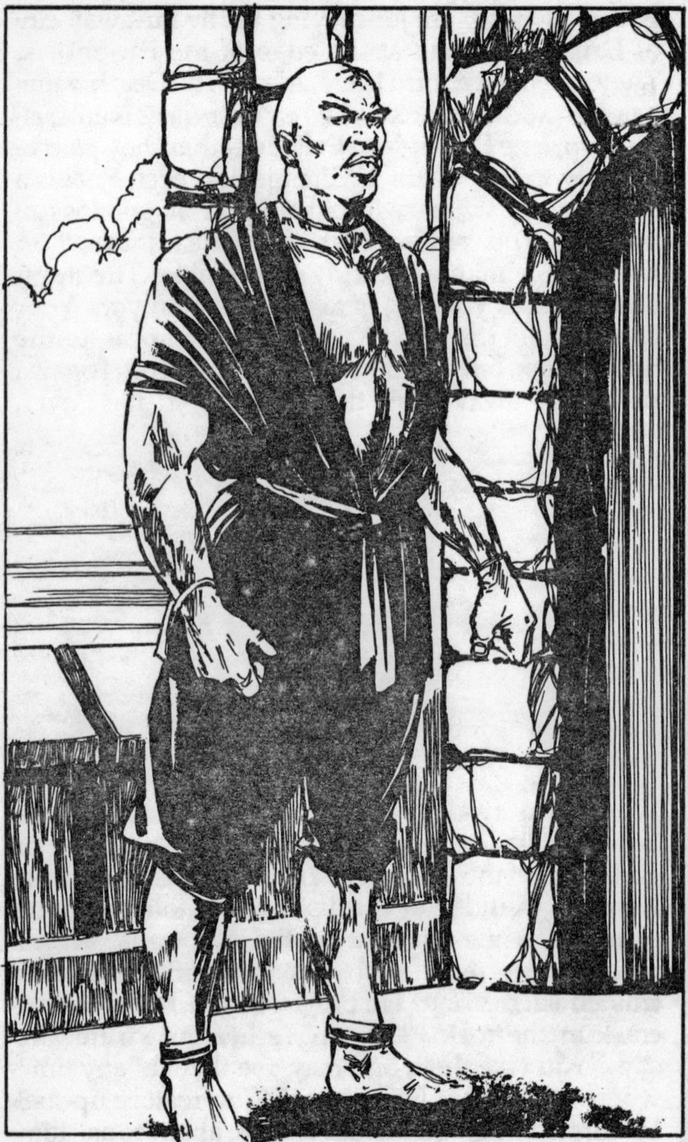

if he will accompany you, when he lies down on the cave floor and falls asleep. Sensing that there is no further help to be gained, you begin the climb down Mount Gwalodrun to the pass below. A day later, you enter the foothills of Fortune Pass. Turn to **70**.

305

Honoric and Manse the Deathmage both lie dead, but your mission is not yet completed. It still remains for you to avenge your spiritual father and kill Yaemon, Grandmaster of Flame, of the order of the Scarlet Mantis. If you fail he will speak the word of power at the Pillars of Change that will bind Kwon in Inferno. You walk down to the roof of the Great Keep. Turn to **101**.

306

Yaemon steps forward and launches a Leaping Tiger kick at your face but you step aside and turn sideways away from his kick. Yaemon's strike whistles past your back as you drive the side of your foot at Yaemon's stomach and then whip it up to his head. He reacts quickly and blocks your first strike with his forearm, but your second strike takes him by surprise and slams into his face. His head swings back as he staggers, momentarily stunned. Subtract 6 from his Endurance. Double this if you used Inner Force. If you have killed Yaemon, turn to **420**. If he is still alive, he is recovering and you may follow up your attack. Will you try the Forked Lightning Strike again (turn to **150**), the Leaping Tiger kick (turn to **278**), the Winged Horse kick (turn to **84**), Kwon's Flail, if you know it (turn to **240**), a punch (turn to **266**) or a throw (turn to **401**)?

307

You enter the Black Sword tavern, a long drinking hall with a blazing fire, even at Harvest time, the month of All-Mother Splendour. There are forty or so drinkers, all men and mostly soldiers. There is not a single sailor to be seen even though you are still close to the harbour. The soldiers have brought their weapons into the tavern but many have loosened or discarded parts of their armour in the sweltering heat. The reek of stale sweat is overpowering. A man who must weigh twenty stones or more ambles up and down the long bar, slamming mugs of mead on the counter and pocketing silver. You buy a mugful and listen to the conversations. They are shouting from table to table about the campaign they are going to fight against the people of the Spires of Foreshadowing. At one table a man of twenty-five or so is particularly loud. He demands mead and two of the soldiers with him grab his mug, fighting for the privilege of buying his drink. He ignores this and, spotting you, challenges you to a drinking bout. Do you accept (turn to **194**) or decline (turn to **186**)?

308

He chops his right hand at the left side of your neck. You bring your leg up in an arc from left to right, sweeping his arm aside but he pulls it back and chops again at the other side of your neck, stunning you. With unrelenting ferocity, Yaemon closes his hand into a fist and snaps his arm straight, bringing his knuckles down sharply on the bridge of your nose and pain washes over you. Barely moments later he slams his foot into your head in a Winged Horse kick, and you are lifted off your feet and hurled backwards, your arms spread wide. Lose 10

Endurance, as the sound of his shouts echo into the night.

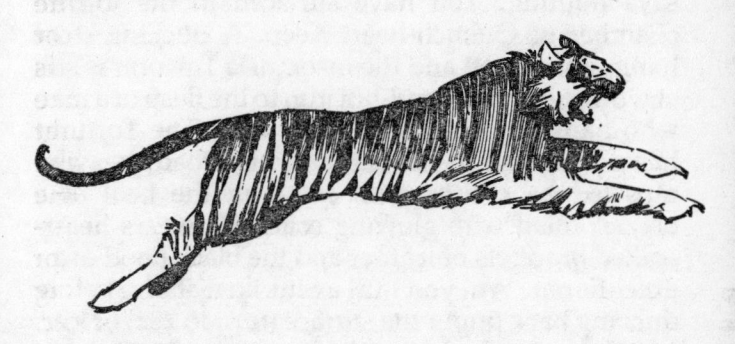

If you are still alive, you manage to break your fall with your arms as you land flat on your back. At the last instant your head clears in time to see Yaemon's foot stamping down at your head and you roll aside and away, springing to your feet, out of range. Warily you circle him and then charge in to the attack. Will you try a punch (turn to **266**), kick (turn to **390**) or throw (turn to **401**)?

309

You have slain an immortal, delivering Orb from one of the beasts which roamed the world before man came from the stars. Breathing deeply but silently, you pass by the fallen hulk to the edge of the inky black underground river which fills the castle moat. The only way onwards is to plunge into the icy waters. You slip into the water and dive down into the chill depths and find that your head hits rock above you before you have surfaced. You swim powerfully along the underwater tunnel for a minute before light shimmering above lets you know that you can surface at last. As you do so, a man's screaming fills your ears. A young boy chained to the wall goggles wide-eyed at you, but says nothing. You have surfaced in the torture chamber of Quench-heart Keep. A ducking stool hangs above you and the insomniac Torturer is still at work, applying a red-hot iron to the flesh of a man who hangs by chains from the roof. The Torturer has a large axe in his belt and his broad, heavily-muscled back runs with sweat in the heat of a brazier filled with glowing coals. He wears heavy spiked bracelets of leather and the black hood of an executioner. Will you hurl a Shuriken at him before ducking back under the surface (turn to **282**) or leap out of the water and attack him (turn to **291**)?

310

Your clenched fist audibly parts the air as you drive it towards the Ogre's body.

> OGRE
> Defence against punch: 4
> Endurance: 16
> Damage: 2 Die

If you have defeated the Ogre, turn to **360**.

If the Ogre is still alive, he tries to crush you with his spiked hammer. Your Defence against his ponderous blow is 8.

If you are still alive, you can now spin sideways and use the Winged Horse kick (turn to **332**), try to sweep the Ogre's legs from under him with the Dragon's Tail throw (turn to **345**) or use the Iron Fist again (return to the top of this paragraph).

311

The small dart speeds past his ear, and the ma-

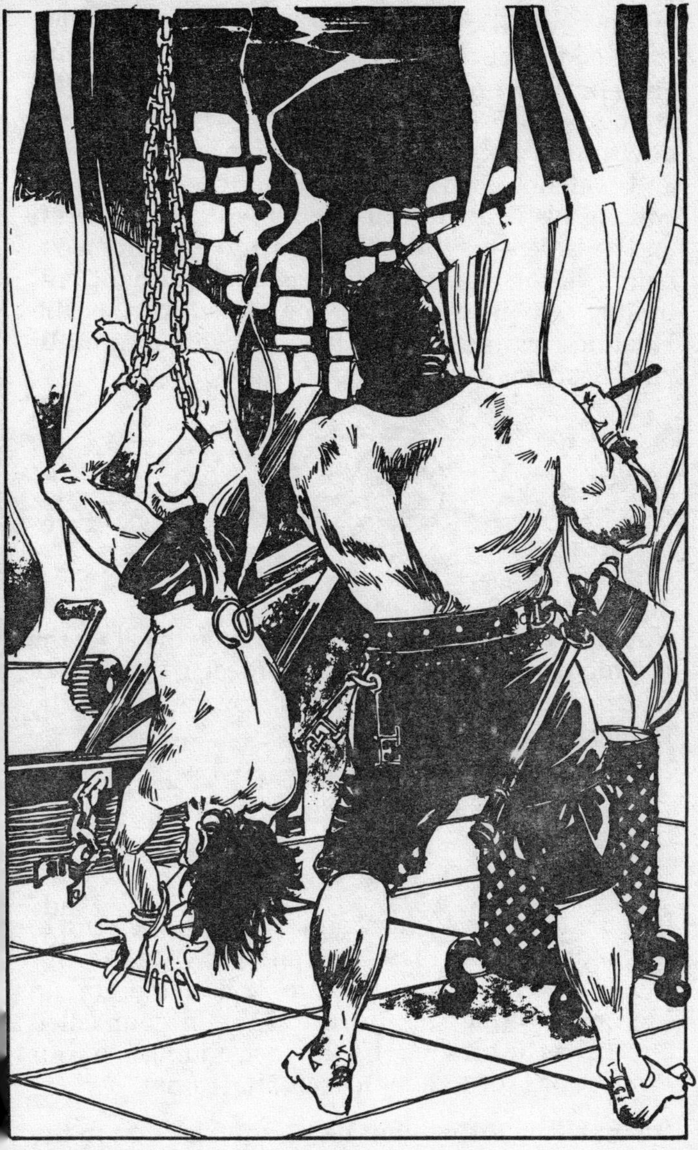

gician's eyes widen in surprise. As you prepare this time to kick the magician he points his finger at you and speaks words which seem to leech you of your strength. You totter feebly as the Hobgoblin bounds down from his castle tower. The magician retreats and watches as the Hobgoblin advances on you, waving his trident. You are too weak even to run and he drives the trident's barbs into your stomach, before lifting you on the tines of the trident and trailing you in the moat. The water boils as the Floating Mouths come to feed and within minutes your flesh has been stripped to the bone.

312

You dart in as if to punch but leap into the air at the last moment, trying to bring your feet to the sides of his head, before twisting and throwing him to the ground.

FIRST REVERENCER OF VILE
Defence against Teeth of the Tiger Throw: 6
Endurance: 15
Damage: 1 Die + 1

If you succeed, you twist and send him spinning to the floor, and then land on your feet. You may try the Tiger's Paw chop (turn to 322) or the Forked Lightning Strike kick (turn to 335) on your fallen attacker as he tries to roll to his feet, adding 1 to your Punch or Kick Modifier for this attack only.

If you fail to throw him, he tries to kick you in the

back as you drop nimbly to your feet. Your Defence against his kick is 6. If you are still alive you may now try the Tiger's Paw chop (turn to **322**) or the Forked Lightning Strike kick (turn to **335**).

313
It is many days march across the snow wastes and not knowing exactly where the city lies, you curse the barren emptiness for there is no clue as to which way to turn. At last you sight the white domes and ice-houses of the City of Far Snows on the eve of a night on which the moon turns red, a night which has no end. You are too late. The eternal darkness has come and Kwon has been imprisoned in Inferno. Your Inner Force drains away and there is nothing you can do to stop the rise of evil. You have failed.

314
You turn down a side street so that you can approach the Hall of Webs from the back and, covered in black from head to toe in your Ninja costume, slink stealthily through the night, your breathing as quiet as a bird's. You stop absolutely still as you catch sight of a monk coming down the otherwise deserted street towards you. He too stops, seeming to sense danger. Are you skilful with Poison Needle Darts? If you are and would like to use one, turn to **329**. Otherwise, turn to **334**.

315
The Cobra Man looks up as you launch yourself into

a flying Leaping Tiger kick. The Cobra Man can strike with the speed of a snake however and his Defence against your kick is 6. If you hit the Cobra Man, turn to **227**. If you fail to kick him, the Cobra Man bites your ankle, injecting a deadly venom. If you do not have Immunity to Poisons, you die painfully. If you do, however, the men goggle in surprise as you pick yourself up while the boy scrambles to safety. Turn to **227**.

316

The Two-headed Giant is dull-witted and slow, but very strong. You will need to strike it several telling blows whilst avoiding the colossal club with which it is trying to flatten you.

TWO-HEADED GIANT
Defence against Leaping Tiger Kick: 4
Endurance: 25
Damage: 2 Dice + 1

If you win, turn to **336**. Your Defence against the monster's tree trunk is 8. It is impossible to Block due to its enormous size and weight, but relatively easy to dodge, due to your comparative smallness and speed, as you try to flip, leap and cartwheel out of its path. If you survive the attack will you use the Iron Fist punch (turn to **325**), the Whirlpool throw (turn to **295**) or kick again (return to the top of this paragraph)?

317

The door swings open easily on its oiled hinges and you glide silently into the chamber. You feel the shadow of fear which comes from Honoric's sword Sorcerak which suddenly speaks his name. Amazingly, he is awake immediately, rolling off the far side of the bed as he clutches the sword. You hurdle the bed but he is ready for you and he shouts out loud as battle royal begins. He grunts with pain as you lash your foot into his side, but he is a hard man and his skill with the sword is breathtaking. He shears clean through your sleeve irons and your left arm is broken and useless but you reply with a great punch which knocks him backwards. Fear shows on Honoric's face as he comprehends your deadliness, but he attacks with new ferocity. Without warning you are felled by a blow from behind and, looking up you see Yaemon's impassive face as Honoric's blade pierces your heart, ending your life.

318

The Barbarian has worked himself into a berserk frenzy of battle lust, cleaving the air with mighty sweeps of his sword, heedless of pain, wanting only your blood. The Dragon's Tail takes him by surprise as you try and sweep his legs from under him. His Defence is only 4 as his sword cuts the air above you.

If you throw him successfully, you may punch (turn to **377**) or kick (turn to **302**) Olvar as he tries to rise, adding 2 to your Punch or Kick Modifier.

If you have failed to throw him, he tries to cut you in half from brow to belly as you get up. Your Defence against this cut as he vents a bloodcurdling roar, is 6 and he does 1 Die + 2 of Damage.

If you survive, you may now kick (turn to **302**) or punch (turn to **377**).

319

As you are about to drop to the ground and sweep his legs from under him, Yaemon unleashes a Winged Horse kick at your head. Acting instinctively, your hands close around his foot. Using a variation of the Dragon's Tail throw, you hook the heel of your right foot around his other ankle and pull it from under him. He falls to the ground and sits up, preparing to twist aside. Still holding his leg, you drive the ball of your right foot into his face with a shout. He loses 6 Endurance. You may double this if you are using Inner Force. If this attack has killed him turn to **420**. If he is still alive, as the top half of his body is driven back to the ground he uses this momentum to wrench his foot from your grasp and somersault backwards, using his hands to propel him into the air and flips onto his feet. Almost immediately, he executes a scissor-kick, his left foot lashes at your groin and his right foot whips straight up at your head, taking him into the air. You step back onto your left foot, with your knees slightly bent and drive the palm of your right hand down in a straight arm block, stopping short Yaemon's kick to the groin, and then bring your arm up across your chest sweeping the kick to your face aside and leaving yourself ready to counter-attack. Will you try the Dragon's Tail throw again (turn to **245**), the Whirlpool throw (turn to **367**), a punch (turn to **266**) or a kick (turn to **390**)?

320

You cross the roof of the Great Keep until you are below the turret which flies the flag of the Sword of

Doom, then climb upwards, silent as a mouse. The staircase within is lit by several torches fixed in brass brackets on the wall and at its top is a heavy oak door. Above the door is a narrow space, just large enough for you to crawl through, which leads to a dank attic. Will you carefully oil the hinges of the door before opening it (turn to **274**) or examine the attic to see if you can spy on the occupant of the chamber beyond (turn to **265**)?

321

As you step forward to punch, the beast lowers its head to charge you, bellowing ferociously. You are meeting the giant immortal head on.

THE ELDER GOD
Defence against Iron Fist: 5
Endurance: 22
Damage: 2 Dice + 2

If you win, turn to **309**. If this creature from the forgotten past still survives, it tries to disembowel you with a flick of its head as it falls briefly onto all fours. Your Defence against this is 6. If you survive, you may use the Winged Horse kick (turn to **333**), the Dragon's Tail throw (turn to **349**) or the Iron Fist again (return to the top of this paragraph).

322

Without warning you raise your hands and try to chop them together on either side of your opponent's neck.

FIRST REVERENCER OF VILE
Defence against Tiger's Paw chop: 6
Endurance: 16
Damage: 1 Die

If you win, turn to **279**. If he is still alive he counters your double Tiger's Paw chop so swiftly that you may not block, as he ducks down and Cobra Strike kicks upwards toward your solar plexus. Your Defence against this jab is 6. If you are still alive you may use the Teeth of the Tiger throw (turn to **312**), the Forked Lightning Strike kick (turn to **335**) or punch again (return to the top of this paragraph).

323

You take some fish scales from one of your pockets and place them on your eyeballs. You can see through them reasonably well but they give you the appearance of a blind man. Sitting down to beg near the entrance to the monastery, you overhear enough to convince you that the monks who worship Vile are steeped in evil, but it is a woman in a black cloak which is covered in the pattern of green spiders' webs who most claims your attention. She is walking towards the monastery flanked by two monks dressed in scarlet, and it seems they are having an argument. She is bartering a price for a spell which they wish her to cast in the 'Hall of Webs'. She is pointing out that if this is their only defence against spies in the corridor which joins the refectory to the sleeping quarters then the Webs of Nullaq spell is worth more than three hundred golds. You pick up your hood with its meagre haul of copper coins and pad slowly away before lying low until darkness falls. You decide to take advantage of your knowledge that the Hall of Webs has only one trap, the webs of the witch you saw earlier. Do you have the Climbing skill? If you do turn to **414**. If you do not, or prefer not to climb in, turn to **314**.

324

As you strike the last monk with what you expect will be the killing blow, strength borne of desperate fear enables him to block the blow at the last moment and he throws himself under the ox-cart, to the other side. He limps away into a nearby building and you decide to leave the city by the north gate before he can call up reinforcements. Turn to **289**.

325

The cumbersome Giant is slow but very strong. You will need to strike several blows to fell it, avoiding the tree-trunk club while you do so.

TWO-HEADED GIANT
Defence against Iron Fist Punch: 3
Endurance: 25
Damage: 2 Dice + 1

If you win, turn to **336**. Your Defence against the colossal club is 8. It is impossible to Block due to its enormous size and weight, but relatively easy to dodge, due to your comparative smallness and speed, as you try to flip, leap and cartwheel out of its path. If you survive the attack will you use the Leaping Tiger kick (turn to **316**), the Whirlpool throw (turn to **295**) or punch again (return to the top of this paragraph)?

326

You slam your fist towards the magician's midriff, but he touches the golden disk which hangs at his chest and the air around him takes on a greenish tinge. He has created some sort of magical shield, and it slows your blow. His Defence against your punch is 6. If you succeed in hitting him turn to **253**. If the field of force stops your blow turn to **311**.

327

You punch again and again but the Shaggoth seems unmoved. It loops its tentacles around you and begins to descend into the swamp once more. You are pulled down with it and slime fills your lungs. It will plant its children in your body, and when they grow you will be their food.

328

You jump up and swing into the hole which leads to the attic, and squeeze through onto the planks beyond. Testing for loose boards, you crawl carefully to a crack in the ceiling. A single candle burning in the chamber below gives just enough light to see by. Honoric is asleep, his arrogant features seem less cruel than in his waking hours and his mouth is open as he snores gently. His great sword lies unsheathed beside him. You cannot spot any traps in the chamber. If you would like to pour your single dose of Blood of Nil poison down a waxed string into Honoric's mouth turn to **158**. If you prefer to get back down to the staircase and go in through the door after oiling its hinges turn to **274**.

329

You make an 'O' shape with your tongue and place one of the poison needles carefully within it in one deft movement. You exhale and spit it out. The needle has imbedded itself in the monk's eye before he realises what you are doing. The poison takes effect. He doubles up, convulsing in the muddy road and dies. Wasting no time, you strip him of his scarlet uniform and put it on over your Ninja costume. Walking with calm assurance you enter the sleeping quarters of the monastery unchallenged and make your way to the Hall of Webs. Turn to **368**.

330

You drive your right fist toward Yaemon's head, but he steps towards you and to the right, legs apart and knees bent, sweeping the side of his left hand up into the inside of your right wrist, pushing your punch past him, and twists his right fist up into your midriff with a shout. You double up. Lose 4 Endurance. If you are still alive, he pulls back his fist and then passes it through the air at your head. You react fast, however, and literally sit down hard as his arm whistles past overhead and then somersault backwards out of range. Rolling into a headstand, you flip to your feet and turn to face Yaemon. He snarls in frustration at your narrow escape. You can attack again. Will you use the Cobra Strike punch (turn to **340**), the Tiger's Paw chop (turn to **410**), a throw (turn to **401**) or a kick (turn to **390**)?

331

As the wind whistles around the turrets of the Great Keep there is a sudden keening howl. For an instant the hairs on the back of your neck prickle with fear, until you realise that it is only the wind howling through an arrow-slit in one of the turrets. The Captain looks startled and you choose this moment to steal up behind him as he moves towards the edge of the roof. You use the Winged Horse kick to tumble him over the battlements and he is falling long before he has realised what has happened. When he does he lets out a piercing shriek of alarm and calls 'Intruder', before hitting the flagstones below with a crash. As you pull back from the edge and make for one of the turrets, light floods the roof area and, looking up, you see Manse the Deathmage. There is a twisted smile on his face as he casts a spell which sends you into a helpless shaking fit. Honoric bursts from the door of his turret and you are helpless as the Marshal of the Legion of the Sword of Doom cuts your head cleanly from your shoulders.

332

You spin and drive the outside of your foot towards the Ogre's purple veined throat as it tries to swat you aside with its hammer.

OGRE
Defence against kick: 5
Endurance: 16
Damage: 2 Dice

If you have defeated the Ogre, turn to **360**.

If the Ogre still lives, it tries to bludgeon your head with its heavy hammer. Your Defence against its clumsy blow is 7.

If you are still alive, you can use the Iron Fist punch (turn to **310**), the Dragon's Tail throw (turn to **345**) or kick again (return to the top of this paragraph).

333

The beast tries to grab you in a crushing embrace but you somersault towards it, under its grasping hands, and roll to your feet, delivering a Winged Horse kick as you do so.

THE ELDER GOD
Defence against Winged Horse: 5
Endurance: 26
Damage: 2 Dice + 2

If you kill the beast, turn to **309**. If the beast is still alive it tries to grab you and impale you on its great horn. Your Defence against this is 7 as you try to leap back beyond its long reach.

If you survive you may use the Iron Fist (turn to **321**), the Dragon's Tail throw (turn to **349**) or kick again (return to the top of this paragraph).

334
To your dismay the moon chooses this moment to come out from behind a cloud and the monk catches sight of your shadow. 'Who are you?' he asks tensely. Will you walk up to him and attack (turn to **359**) or use a Shuriken (turn to **347**)?

335
Without a flicker of muscle to announce your intent until you are moving, you move to the right and side-kick twice in quick succession, once to the side of his left knee and then up to the left side of his head, catching him by surprise.

FIRST REVERENCER OF VILE
Defence against Forked Lightning Strike kick: 6
Endurance: 16
Damage: 1 Die + 1

If you win, turn to **279**. If the monk is still alive he feints a punch and then drives his heel towards your

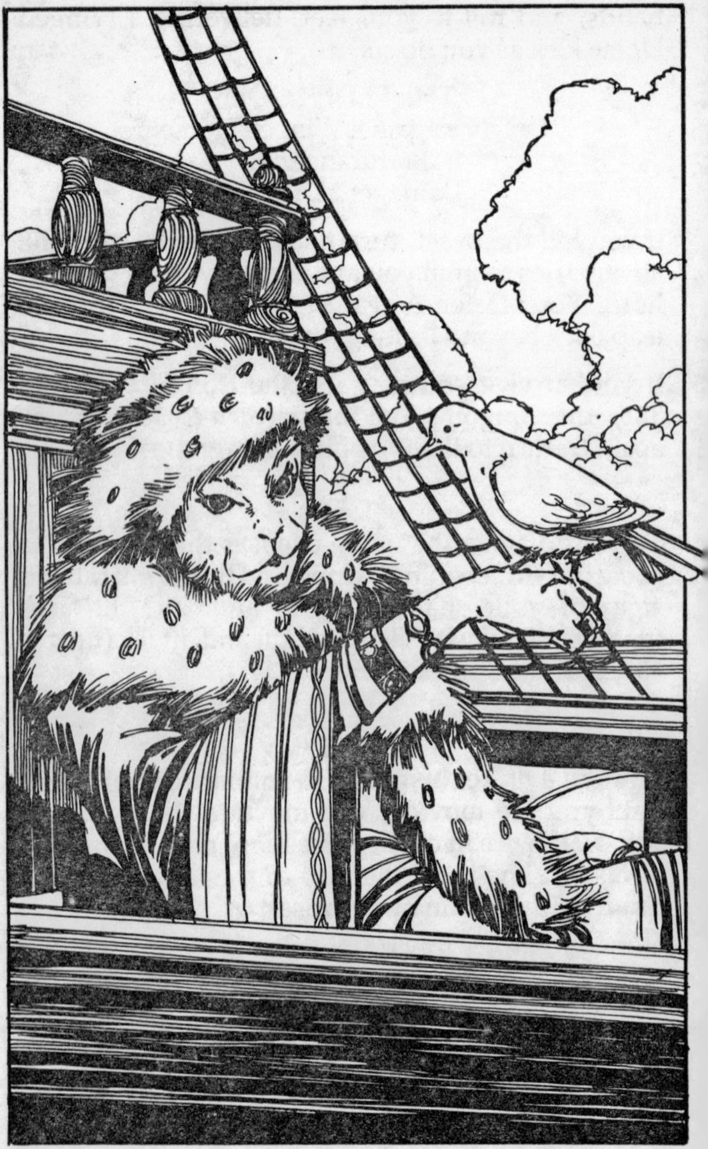

neck. Your Defence against his kick is 7. If you are still alive you may use the Teeth of the Tiger throw (turn to **312**), the Tiger's Paw chop (turn to **322**) or kick again (return to the top of this paragraph).

336

The Two-headed Giant crashes to the ground, cracking the rock. Saliva flecked with blood covers its lips. You move on, and in the mist see the cave which was its lair. Investigating carefully you find a selection of bones, cracked open, which have had the marrow sucked out of them, and a small sack full of copper pieces. The Giant's treasure is worthless to you, too heavy to carry, but you do find a black leather gauntlet sewn with delicate silver thread. It carries the virtue of magic, a Gauntlet of Striking and you put it on. Add + 1 to your Punch Modifier when using the Iron Fist, Tiger's Paw or Cobra Strike punches. You continue on through the hills as the mist lifts and head into the wild wastelands towards the city of Fiendil. Turn to **93**.

337

The ship is rowed out of the harbour and the sail unfurled. You stand at the rail looking back at the receding cliffs. There is only one other passenger, a woman swathed against the sea breeze in ermine who seems to fascinate the crew. She seeks you out, introducing herself as Dierdra and looking around you see that her face is painted so that she resembles an exquisite cat. You have never seen such face paint and the unnaturalness disturbs you. She smiles and asks if you find the journey tedious. You do not reply but she goes on, 'I would not bother, myself, if I were not going to entertain someone who interests me.' You begin to talk to her, for some time, and she tells you that she is a singer, but it is when she talks of those who are to be her audience that you become most interested. From her description it can only be Yaemon, Grandmaster of Flame, the man you have sworn to kill. She talks too, of the man called Manse the Deathmage, a black sorcerer who reveres Nemesis, and can summon beings from the elemental planes to fight his enemies. She does not seem perturbed at the idea of meeting such people but soon her pleasantly lilting voice has you spellbound. Before you realise what you are doing you have told her of your quest. Sick with fear you wait to see her reaction as the spell of enchantment is broken. She smiles and says that she is not really a singer at all, but an enchantress and swears by all that is good that she will help you. She turns away and coos softly twice. A white dove appears in the sky behind you and flies down to land on her outstretched hand. As the ship glides into the harbour at Druath Glennan she tells you to visit the house of a poor family outside the city wall and wait there for word from her. Unsure whether you are doing as she bids you because you trust her, or because she has enchanted you, you disembark from the ship and walk towards the tumbledown shack that seems to cower in the shadow beneath the city wall. Turn to **300**.

338

The needle buries itself in the magician's cheek and he claps a hand to it as the deadly poison takes effect. He begins to rock on his feet and then topples into the moat. The crowd are hushed for they were not able to see the needle and they think you are a warlock. The water boils as the Floating Mouths latch onto their prey. Within a minute his flesh has been stripped to the bone. You climb up towards the Hobgoblin in his tower. The beast is showing off to the crowd, confident of another victory, beating his chest which is twice as broad as yours and twisting the trident in one hand. The tower is roughly built, with many hand-holds and you move around it, keeping the Hobgoblin confused as to your precise position. Then, holding an outcrop of stone with your hands, you swing up into the tower behind him. He whirls and you attack him with blinding speed. Will you use the Leaping Tiger kick (turn to 281), the Whirlpool throw (turn to 267) or the Tiger's Paw chop (turn to 293)?

339

You enter the turret and glide soundlessly upwards. The staircase is lit by several torches fixed in brass brackets on the wall and, wary of traps, you make no more noise than a cat stalking a bird. At the top of the turret beyond a single window is a heavy oak door. Above the door is a narrow space, just large enough for you to crawl through, which leads to a dank attic. Will you carefully oil the hinges of the door before opening it (turn to 317) or examine the attic to see if you can spy on the occupant of the chamber beyond (turn to 328)?

340

As you step forward, Yaemon lashes his fist out towards your head, but you drop to one knee and drive a straight fingered jab up into his midriff, just under his rib-cage. He grunts in pain and doubles up. You spring to your feet, whipping your elbow up, so that your right hand rests on your right shoulder, cracking him sharply under the jaw. Subtract 4 from his Endurance; you may double this if you are using Inner Force. If he is dead, turn to **420**. If he still lives, his head snaps back, but he executes a backward flip, bringing his feet up towards your face which you just manage to avoid, and then up over his head, and lands safely some feet away. However, you are close behind him and may attack again. Will you try the Cobra Strike punch again (turn to **301**), the Iron Fist punch (turn to **330**), the Tiger's Paw chop (turn to **410**), a kick (turn to **390**) or a throw (turn to **401**)?

341

You strike north from Doomover until you come to a marshland called the Greenfen. You skirt this, crossing the river which flows out of the dank mires and trot for a few days, hunting and foraging at need and sleeping in trees. After several days you turn north east and warily cross the track which leads north from Mortavalon to the city of Sundial and climb into the wild and windswept hills known as the Barrow Swales, heading for the city of Fiendil. You may restore any Endurance lost so far on this journey. On a day which dawns strangely cold, a mist lies heavily around the hills and you find yourself in a narrow gully. A boulder thuds dully towards you from higher up the hill but you leap agilely out of its way, to be faced by a great Two-headed Giant waving a thorny club, which looks like the trunk of a small tree. The club whistles through the air towards you and you duck low beneath it. The Giant roars in frustration. Will you use the Leaping Tiger kick (turn to **316**), the Iron Fist punch (turn to **325**) or the Whirlpool throw (turn to **295**)?

342

He leans forward as you thrust up the rope towards

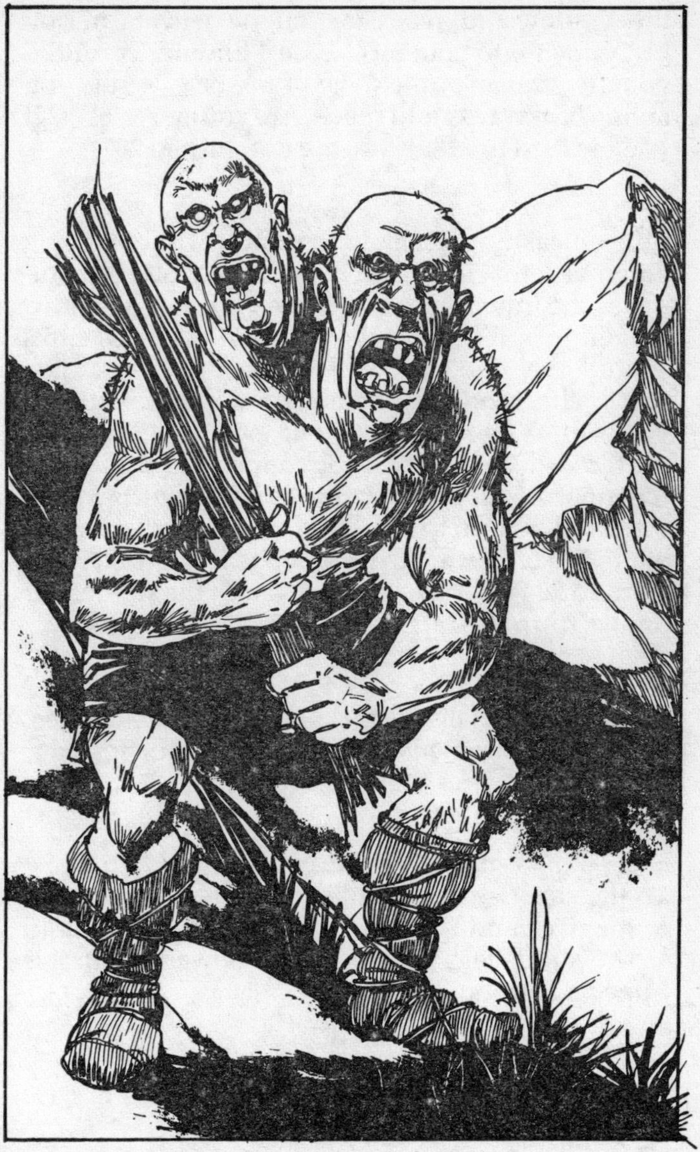

the window and, ready for you, he delivers an Iron Fist punch into your face. Lose 4 Endurance, and if you are still alive, the force of the blow sends you falling backwards into space. Are you an Acrobat? If you are turn to **298**. If you are not, turn to **287**.

343

You unleash a tremendous punch at the heaving green sack that is the body of the Shaggoth, screaming as the Inner Force leaves you. It is racked with a quivering and its tentacles fall from you, as it sinks soundlessly into the bubbling swamp. Seeing this, the Troll behind you shambles away from you and you continue your difficult journey. By nightfall you are through the fens and you continue by the light of the moon. At sunup you must decide which way to turn. Will you go to Ionalbion on the southern coast of the Sea of the Star to take ship to Druath Glennan (turn to **294**) or strike north towards the City of Far Snows (turn to **313**)?

344

The Barbarian falls at last, a mass of broken bones. At the end it seemed that he would fight on for ever, but his battle cries will no longer trouble the world of Orb. Turn to **366**.

345

To the surprise of the dull-witted Ogre you crouch to the deck and try to sweep its legs from under it. However, its legs are stocky and powerful and it is huge and strong.

OGRE
Defence against throw: 8
Endurance: 16
Damage: 2 Dice

If you succeed, you may use a kick (turn to **332**) or a punch (turn to **310**), adding 2 to your Kick or Punch Modifier for this attack only.

If you have failed to bring the Ogre crashing to the deck it tries to drive you through it with its hammer. Your Defence against the falling hammer is 7 as you try to roll backwards into a handstand and then flip onto your feet. You have no time to block the heavy blow.

If you are still alive you may now use the Iron Fist punch (turn to **310**) or the Winged Horse kick (turn to **332**).

346

After a short while fiddling with a small piece of wire, the lock slides back and you step through the gate into the hallway of the Keep and, when you hear footsteps approaching inside, you quickly close the gate. Without a moment's hesitation you cross to the far corner of the wall and, jumping up, wedge yourself between the ceiling and the two walls. You hang there for twenty minutes while the Bailiff and a guard who have appeared below you plan a raid on the wine-cellar. At last they disappear and, dropping to the floor, you massage life back into your numb limbs, before climbing the spiral staircase, which is at the opposite side of the hall. Half way up, your keen sight notices a network of fine threads stretched across the staircase and connected to wires which disappear through holes in the inner wall. You stand on your hands and 'walk' up the staircase, feeling for the near invisible threads as you go and straining your ears for the slightest sound. At last you are past them. Turn to **399**.

347

The Shuriken hurtles towards him, glinting in the moonlight. He tries to dodge aside but it catches him in the arm, instead of the throat as you had intended. He cries the alarm and falls back, clutching his arm. You will not be able to retrieve the Shuriken – cross it off your Character Sheet. You decide that to remain would imperil your mission and lose yourself quickly in the side streets, lying low in a burnt-out bakery for the night. You reflect that the monk may have recognised you were a Ninja and decide to leave Doomover, intent on making sure that Yaemon does not arrive at the Pillars of Change before you. Using the disguise of a beggar, you leave the city in the morning. Turn to **254**.

348

You cross the roof of the Great Keep and enter the turret which boasts the Scarlet Mantis banner. Gliding silently up the dark staircase, you feel your way carefully, testing for traps. There are none and soon your ear is at the door to the chamber at the top of the stone steps. You can hear nothing inside the room and you oil the hinges of the oak door before sliding it gently open. Yaemon, Grandmaster of Flame of the order of the Scarlet Mantis is within, meditating cross-legged on the floor. He is wearing the scarlet fighting dress of a martial arts monk, and a black cotton belt. A shout of surprise escapes him as he stands up. Then his face stern and impassive once more, he bows to you. 'Welcome, Ninja, you are Avenger. I killed your spiritual father,' he says. You bow in turn and leap to the attack. Yaemon proves himself to be a peerless fighter, kicking, punching and blocking with dazzling speed and power, but your controlled hatred spurs you to great feats. Yaemon is hard-pressed until you hear footsteps on the staircase below. Honoric has answered Yaemon's shout and he bursts in behind you waving his smoking blade, Sorcerak. You resist the fear which emanates from the Eldritch Sword but you are no match for them both, for they are two of the greatest warriors Orb has ever known. At the last Yaemon's fist smashes into your temple, just as Sorcerak severs your neck and your head bounces around the room, like a bladder-ball.

You have failed and no-one can stop these men now. Evil will rule the world.

349

You slide beneath its feet but cannot move its colossal legs. Instead it collapses on top of you, driving the breath from your body and crushing your ribcage. Suddenly, the beast, whose sense of smell is acute, lunges and impales you on its horn with its massively powerful arms. You are still twitching feebly as it begins to feed on the entrails which have spilled from your body.

350

As he flies towards you, you flip backwards into a handstand and then bounce backwards onto your feet again several times, moving out of range of Yaemon's attack. As he is coming down, you reverse direction and flip towards him with great speed, coming to a stop before him, just as he lands agilely on his feet. You have the chance to attack. Will you punch (turn to **266**), throw (turn to **401**) or kick (turn to **390**)?

351

Seeing that you will not clasp his hand, the magician begins to chant a spell. If you have the skill of Poison Needles, you may wish to use one (turn to **389**) or you may wish to attack him with an Iron Fist punch (turn to **326**).

352

You run a few steps along the Aquamarin's deck before leaping the rail and landing against the side of the pirate ship, hanging from the scuppers by your hands. You wait for a moment before edging your way, hand over hand, towards the red stern of the Watery Grave. Make a Fate Roll to see if one of the Reavers spotted you jumping onto their ship. If Fate smiles on you, turn to **107**. If Fate turns her back on you, turn to **97**.

353

You may choose which one to attack but these monks who reverence Vile are well versed in the martial arts. One of the monks tries to use a Winged Horse on you, but you side-step to the left and try to bring your right hand down across his throat with a Tiger's Paw.

	1st Monk	2nd Monk
Defence against		
Tiger's Paw	7	7
Endurance	14	13
Damage	1 Die + 1	1 Die + 1

If you have defeated them, turn to **324**. If they are still alive, they will attack you. Your Defence against their multiple attacks is 6 if both are attacking, and 8 if only one remains alive. If you survive you may use the Winged Horse kick (turn to **374**), the Teeth of the Tiger throw (turn to **286**) or punch again (return to the top of this paragraph).

354

The guard hesitates, then says, 'Wait here while I fetch the necessary papers, you will need a pass.' With that he signals another soldier to take over and walks under the portcullis into the castle bailey. As you stare at his receding back you reflect that Mortavalon is hundreds of miles to the south, a long way to have come since your last performance. But, then, perhaps you can say that you are travelling home to the City of Far Snows. Do you await the guard's return (turn to **31**) or leave in case he is preparing a trap (turn to **15**)?

355

The guards look into the blazing fire which blinds them to everything else around them. One of them mutters, 'Just a log settling in the fire,' whilst you steal silently past them and down the stairway to the Inner Bailey below. A guard is doing the rounds of the inner courtyard but you wait until he is out of sight on the other side of the Great Keep, and glide across the grass like a shade, to a small gate that leads into the Keep itself. Are you a skilled Pick-Lock? If you are, you may try to open the locked gate (turn to **346**). If you do not have this skill or do not choose to use it turn to **381**.

357

The boy screams as he dies and the men crack the whip over their ox and drive off, dragging the Cobra Man behind them. There is a cave, overhung by rock above you in the hillside.

'That way to Mortavalon,' one of the men shouts, pointing to it. Will you continue along the road (turn to **283**) or investigate the cave (turn to **275**)?

358

The monster crouches as you climb the side of the cavern, burying your Cat's Claws into cracks in the roof of the cavern. It is shackled to the wall by links of heavy chain with enough slack to cross to your side of the cavern. Suddenly, the beast, whose sense of smell is acute, lunges towards you, ripping you down from the ceiling and impaling you on its horn with its massively powerful arms. You are still twitching feebly as it begins to feed on the entrails which have spilled from your body.

359

You step towards him and without warning, unleash a Flying Winged Horse kick at his throat. If you decide to use Inner Force, turn to **395**. If you cannot or will not, turn to **403**.

360

The Ogre buckles at the knees and topples backwards between the two ships, a plume of spray rises from where he plummets into the water. If you have used a Shuriken it is lost with the Ogre. Looking quickly around you can see that the Reavers, with their ear-rings and scimitars are more than a match for the crew of the Aquamarin. Glaivas' swordsmanship is startling but they are slowly penning him in. With a punishing sidekick you knock a new attacker to the floor, where he lies inert. Another huge wart-faced Halforc lunges at you with his cutlass. With incredible speed, you clap your hands together, trapping the blade between them, inches from your face. He has time to gape in astonishment before you smash the top of your right foot into his temple. Now will you:

Try to fight your way through to Glaivas (turn to 371)?
Jump to the Reavers' ship to attack the pirate Captain (turn to 352)?

361

All is dark on the inside of the turret, but as you look up to the door at its top you see a red eye, hanging disembodied in space. It glows, and the white of the eye is horribly bloodshot. As you watch, it blinks and then suddenly disappears. Will you listen at the chamber door (turn to 364) or cross the roof of the Great Keep to the turret with the Black Whirlpool flag (turn to 130)?

362

There is nothing you can do as the surface of the

swamp closes above you. Not even the Troll who chased you dares to save you for his supper.

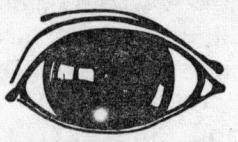

363

As you grasp his hand it tingles and then a shock of electricity galvanises your body. Lose 7 Endurance. If you are still alive, you overcome the pain which would have crippled most people – your training has often brought worse – and use the Iron Fist punch, striking him in the abdomen and then, spinning, use the Winged Horse kick, hammering your foot into his face, catapulting him into the moat. The water boils as the Floating Mouths latch onto their prey. Within a minute his flesh has been stripped to the bone.

You climb up towards the Hobgoblin in his tower. The beast is showing off to the crowd, confident of another victory, beating his chest, which is twice as broad as yours, and twirling the trident in one hand. The tower is roughly built with many hand-holds, and you move around it, keeping the Hobgoblin confused as to your precise position. Then, holding an outcrop of stone with your hands, you swing up into the tower behind him. He whirls round and you attack him with blinding speed. Will you use the Leaping Tiger kick (turn to 281), the Whirlpool throw (turn to 267) or the Tiger's Paw chop (turn to 293)?

364

You can hear nothing inside the room and you oil the hinges of the oak door before sliding it gently open. Yaemon, Grandmaster of Flame of the order of the Scarlet Mantis is within, meditating cross-legged on the floor. He is wearing the scarlet fighting dress of a martial arts monk, and a black cotton belt. His face is stern and impassive as he stands and bows to you.

'Welcome, Ninja, you are Avenger and I killed your spiritual father,' he says. You bow in turn and leap to the attack. Yaemon proves himself to be a peerless fighter, kicking, punching and blocking with dazzling speed and power, but your controlled hatred spurs you to great feats. Yaemon is hard-pressed until you hear footsteps on the staircase below. The red eye was a spell cast by Manse the Deathmage. He saw you through the disembodied eye and summoned the guards, who burst into the chamber behind you. You turn to block a sword thrust but Yaemon throws you to the ground and one of the soldiers pins you to the floorboards with his sword. You have failed your mission.

365

The throwing star misses and embeds itself in the wooden wall of the hut, as the globe of energy hits you and explodes. Lose 6 Endurance as the blast sears you and throws you backwards a few paces. If you are still alive, you snarl in rage as you circle Runeweaver. Turn to **276**.

366

You try to take the Circlet from the Barbarian's head

but burn yourself when you touch it. You see from the Eldritch characters carved upon it that it was forged deep in the Rift by Dark Elves. No one of true heart may touch it.

You spend the night in the hut and may regain up to 3 Endurance points. You leave the useless treasures behind; they would encumber you on your journey, but you do decide to take 5 gold pieces from Olvar that could prove useful and at daybreak set out once more on your mission. Later in the day you descend from the heights of Fortune Pass. Will you head north east to the shores of the Sea of the Star and Druath Glennan (turn to **219**), due north towards the City of Far Snows (turn to **313**), or turn east through the Trollfens to the City of Ionalbion to take ship across the Sea of the Star (turn to **59**)?

367

You lash your left arm out in an attempt to catch Yaemon's wrist, but he reacts almost instantaneously and stepping back and grabbing your arm, he spins you so that your back is facing him. He heaves your forearm up between your shoulder blades in a painful arm-lock, whilst his other arm snakes around your head. Knowing you have only an instant before your neck is broken, you drop into a crouch and jump, bringing your legs up and over Yaemon's head, to land behind him, breaking his hold. However, as your feet hit the ground, he spins around and whips the top of his right foot up in a sweeping arc from right to left. The blow lands on the side of your head with devastating effect as he screams with the power of Inner Force. Lose 10 Endurance. If you are still alive, your reflexes take over, and you roll with the blow, cartwheeling away to Yaemon's side. As you come to a stop, feeling slightly groggy, he is upon you again, with a flurry of blows. If you have Acrobatic skills, turn to **181**. If you do not, you will have to try and block his multiple attack. Your Defence is 7. If you succeed, turn to **118**. If you fail, turn to **308**.

368

The Hall of Webs is an arcing corridor, like a humpback bridge, which connects the upper floor of the dwellings to the refectory where the monks take their meals. The door opens to reveal a room dimly lit by two flickering candles. Forewarned, you notice the glint of many threads as slender as a spider's web, criss-crossing the floor. Some of them, you guess, will be attached to bells or traps which will give you away or kill you. Bending down, you do a handstand and walk carefully into the room on your hands. You are able to balance on one arm whilst with the other you delicately test the floor ahead for strands of web. It takes you half an hour to slowly cross the room but you manage it without breaking any of the strands. You reach the door and, neatly flipping onto your feet, open it soundlessly. You are on the balcony above the refectory and the dining hall. Crouching behind the balcony, you overhear the information you need, as the monks drink wine late into the night. It seems Yaemon has left for Mortavalon, accompanied by Honoric, Marshal of the Legion of the Sword of Doom, a ten-day since. Before you leave, you catch sight of a scroll that details some of the kicks, punches and throws used in the Way of the Mantis, the fighting style of the monks who worship Vile. You may increase your Punch Modifier by one as you learn some useful techniques. They are skilled in punching. You also notice that they have no knowledge of the Forked Lightning Strike. This may be useful to you whenever you must fight a monk who worships Vile. You manage to get out the way you came without difficulty and lie low in a burnt-out bakery for the rest of the night. In the morning, you leave Doomover, intent on catching up with Yaemon and Honoric. Turn to **65**.

369

You place your heel against the gate-lock, and the breath hisses from your lungs as you let the Inner Force explode from you. The lock snaps with a crack and the gate swings open. You step into the Keep and, when you hear footsteps approaching inside, you quickly close the gate. Without a moment's hesitation you cross to the far corner of the wall and, jumping up, wedge yourself between the ceiling and the two walls. You hang there for twenty minutes while the Bailiff and a guard who have appeared below you plan a raid on the wine-cellar. At last they disappear and, dropping to the floor, you massage life back into your numb limbs, before climbing the spiral staircase which is at the opposite side of the hall. Half-way up your keen sight notices a network of fine threads stretched across the staircase and connected to wires which disappear through holes in the inner wall. You stand on your hands and 'walk' up the staircase, feeling for the near invisible threads as you go and straining your ears for the slightest sound. At last you are past them. Turn to **399**.

370

Have you used that most deadly poison, the Blood of Nil? If you have turn to **305**. If you have not turn to **348**.

371

You fight on, felling two more of the swarthy buccaneers. But the crew are rapidly being overpowered, some fools are even surrendering. You are surrounded but no one can close with you past the flashing blows of your fists and feet. Suddenly one of them looks above you and grins. Turning your eyes to the heavens you see the rigging collapsing on you. One of them has shinned up the mast and cut the rigging down. You can hardly move beneath it and a torrent of pirate bodies bears you, struggling, to the ground. You are carried below.

Your Ninja equipment is taken from you and you are roped to one of the Aquamarin's oars. Turn to **19**.

372

The robed man steps towards you, he is young, no older than yourself and his eyes twinkle merrily. A golden disk hangs in front of his chest on a necklace of coral. The Hobgoblin watches, thumping his trident in the castle tower. The young man speaks.

'Greetings, fellow combatant. I will not ask what crime you have committed that the people of Mortavalon sent you into the arena. Instead let me make a suggestion to you. I am a magician, my spells are potent and deadly.' You notice that his golden and blue robes are unruffled as he continues, 'I have killed the Giant of the Snows and I could kill you, but then I would have to kill that too,' he points at the Hobgoblin, 'and if I died, not one of us would have survived. Let us make peace and kill that foul beast together, then let the crowd decide which of us shall live. Here, clasp my hand on it.' He offers his hand. If you wish to accept his hand, either to throw him into the moat or to join him, turn to **363**, or if you would rather attack him in some other way turn to **351**.

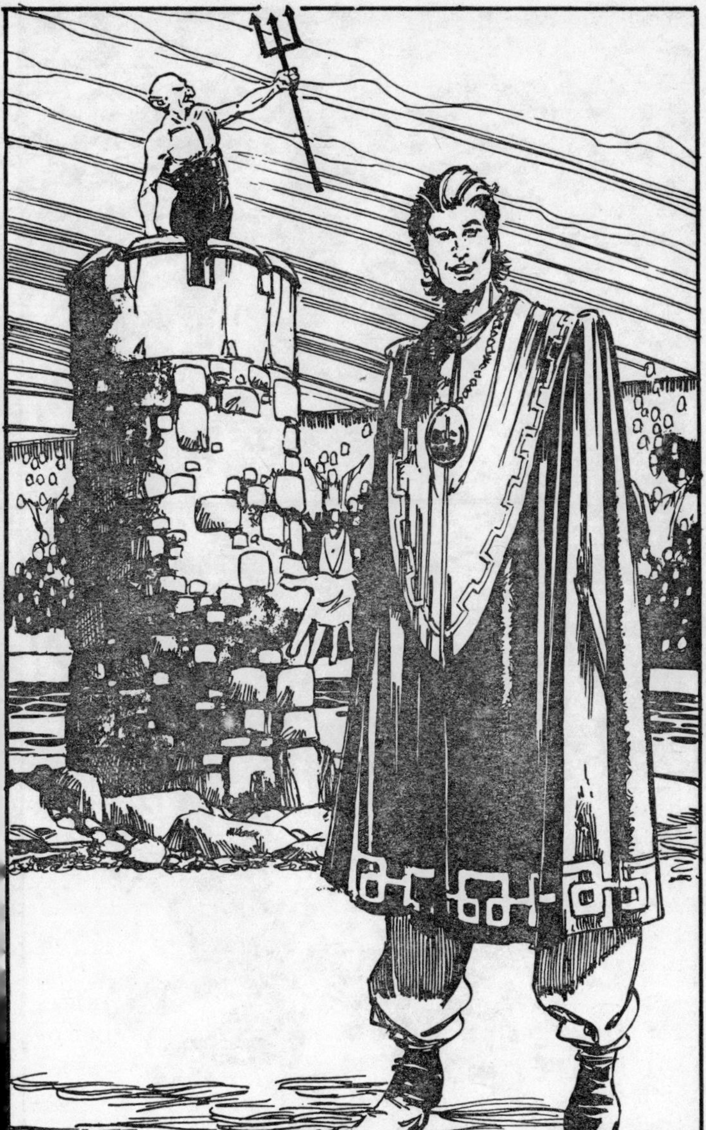

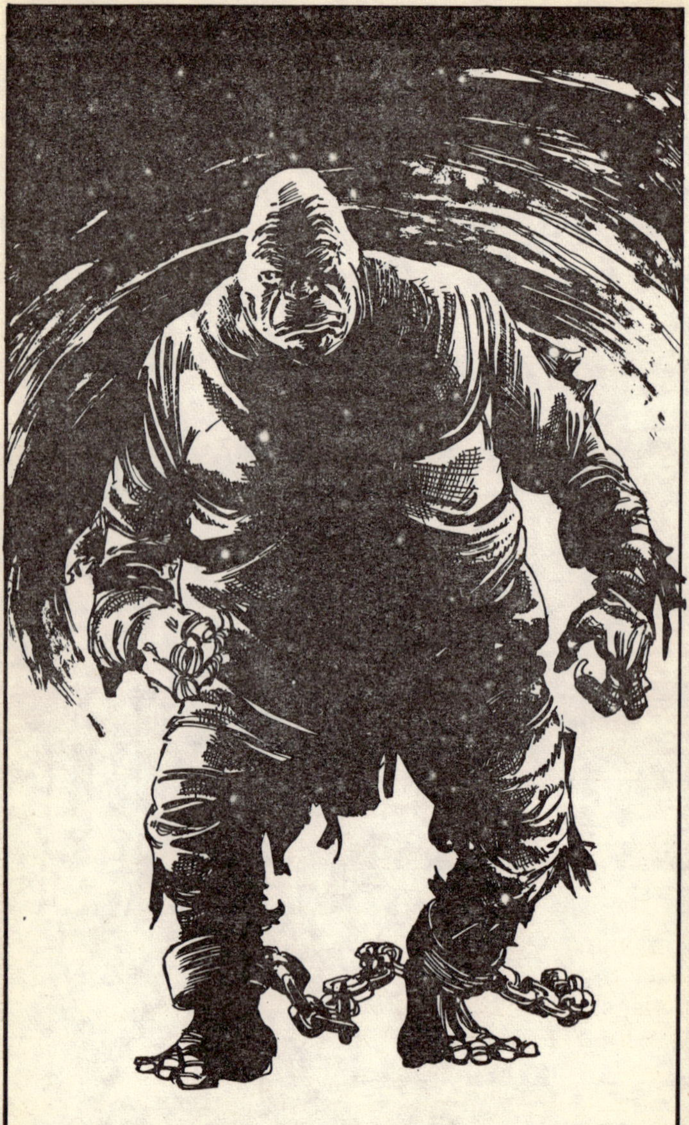

373

The huge monster lumbers towards you and you can see that it resembles a great hairless ape. It is chained at the ankle with massive iron links, so that it can only reach the entrance to the cavern. The great areas of hanging skin reveal enormous black muscles taut with power. Will you use the Winged Horse kick (turn to **333**), the Iron Fist (turn to **321**) or the Dragon's Tail throw (turn to **349**)?

374

You may choose which monk to attack. One of them tries to punch you but you lean back out of range, turn and drive your foot towards his head.

	1st Monk	2nd Monk
Defence against		
Winged Horse	6	7
Endurance	14	13
Damage	1 Die + 1	1 Die + 1

If you have defeated them, turn to **324**. If they are still alive, they will attack you. Your Defence against their flying kicks is 6 if they are both attacking and 8 if only one is still alive. If you are still alive, you may use the Teeth of the Tiger throw (turn to **286**), the Tiger's Paw chop (turn to **353**) or the Winged Horse again (return to the top of this paragraph).

375

You manage to cling to the flints of the Hall of Webs as the monk throws the grappling hook to the flagstone below, and throw your voice, like a ventriloquist, so that the monk hears what he believes is a groan of pain from the courtyard below. He chuckles and then leans out of the window to look down but cannot see in the darkness. He pulls back and you inch slowly up the wall to the window and, pushing off with your feet, swing down and into the window to land silently behind him as he walks from the window. He seems to sense you and is turning his head when you throw your Garotte-wire around his neck. He dies soundlessly. The hall is dimly lit by two flickering candles but your sharp eyesight can see the glinting of webs which crisscross the floor. Reaching up from the window ledge, you bury your Cat's Claws into the plaster ceiling and slowly cross it to the door, hanging upside down, like a fly. You drop to the floor and quietly open the door. You are on the balcony above the refectory and the dining hall. Crouching behind the balcony, you overhear the information you need, as the monks drink wine late into the night. It seems Yaemon has left for Mortavalon, accompanied by Honoric, Marshal of the Legion of the Sword of Doom, a ten-day since. Before you leave, you catch sight of a scroll. that details some of the kicks, punches and throws used in the Way of the Mantis, the fighting style of the monks who worship Vile. You may increase your Throw Modifier by one as you learn some useful techniques and you also notice that they have no knowledge of the Forked Lightning Strike. You manage to get out through a window off the balcony and climb down to the courtyard where you pick up your grappling hook before lying low in a burnt-out bakery for the rest of the night. In the morning, you leave Doomover intent on catching up with Yaemon and Honoric. Turn to **65**.

376

You lie unmoving on the grass as they dismount to examine your body. You stop breathing almost completely and concentrate so that the blood stops flowing to your skin and your heart rate drops to a minimum. When they touch you it seems you are already growing slightly stiff and when, after a few minutes your brow feels cold, they ride off and leave you. As they mount up they are deciding to return to their temple, that of Nemesis, Supreme Principle of Evil.

'Manse will be pleased,' says one.

'Yes, and those strange monks of the Mantis,' says another. When they have left you continue warily, wondering how news of you had travelled ahead so quickly and why the priests of Nemesis should be in league with the monks who worship Vile. After a time you enter the hills that encircle Mortavalon and remember that you have heard of a sorcerer who worships Nemesis, Manse the Deathmage, supposedly one of the most powerful beings on Orb. Your musings are interrupted when you see a cave in the hillside above you. Will you continue along the road to Mortavalon (turn to **283**) or enter the cave (turn to **275**)?

377

Olvar lets out a ferocious cry as, throwing caution to the wind, he whirls his sword above his head and then lunges at you. He is berserk, lost in a battle frenzy. He will feel no fear or pain until either you or he lie dead. Subtract one from any damage you do to him. You parry his blade with your forearm, sidestep and unleash a Cobra Strike from your hip.

OLVAR THE BARBARIAN
Defence against Cobra Strike: 6
Endurance: 18
Damage: 1 Die + 2

235

If you have defeated Olvar, turn to **344**. If he still lives, he swings his sword in a great arc from left to right, trying to cut open your chest. Your Defence against his savage cut is 8 as you try to leap backwards.

If you still live, you may kick (turn to **302**), throw (turn to **318**) or punch again (return to the top of this paragraph).

378

The three Shuriken speed toward Yaemon's throat but with astounding timing he turns sideways and, raising his right forearm in front of his chest, passes his right hand up, down and up through the air in a rapid flailing motion, using the back of his hand and the heel of his palm to deflect the Shuriken, without touching their blades, and they whir away into the night. Amazed as you are, you know you must act before he has finished concentrating on your stars. Will you use a Poison Needle, if you have the skill (turn to **69**) or run to the attack (turn to **89**)?

379

You leap back but stumble down the stairs and the now huge green gem tumbles down on top of you. You find yourself inside it and it carries you down the staircase, rolling out across the roof of the Great Keep. Through the glassy green wall you see Yaemon appear as Manse follows you out onto the Keep's roof. The gem begins to contract and you shrink with it until you are the size of an ant. Manse the Deathmage smiles as he picks the gem up from the floor and you hear him remarking to Yaemon that he will have you mounted in a ring. You will live for a long time, a miniature madman on the hand of the Deathmage.

380

The arrow reaches you as you are in mid-air between the rigging and the deck but you whip your hand up and snatch it out of the air inches before your chest, and throw it aside. The Ogre, enraged, raises its spiked hammer to smash you. Will you:

Try the Winged Horse kick (turn to **332**)?
Attempt the Iron Fist punch (turn to **310**)?
Slide across the deck and use the Dragon's Tail throw (turn to **345**)?

381

If you have climbing skills you may climb up the side of the Keep to its roof (turn to **174**) or climb up the Keep and force an entry at one of the lower windows (turn to **2**). If you do not have this skill, or do not choose to use it, you may, if you have any Inner Force left, try to force the lock open (turn to **369**). Failing this, you cannot find a way into the Keep from the Inner Bailey and you can only try the grille at the moat. You manage the easy climb back up to the top of the derelict tower. Turn to **393**.

382

Your magnificent leap is enough to carry you to the island and you land nimbly on your feet, as the crowd cheers loudly. You look around. The Dark Elf is nowhere to be seen, lost in the swamp, and the knight lies spread-eagled on the sand but the man in blue and gold robes is floating across the moat on a small ice floe. Turn to **372**.

383

As you edge forward a cavern opens out around you and you can see the vague outline of what looks like one of the Elder Gods, in the light of a single smoking torch. A great horn protrudes from its head and it stoops, almost brushing the tip against the fifteen foot high ceiling. Its outline is strangely jagged and the smell of putrefaction suggests that its thick hide is sloughing off in great dead patches. If it is truly one of the Elder Gods you know that it will be immensely strong even if weakened by its existence in this dank pit of slime. The half-eaten corpse of the unfortunate who was fed to the beast as you arrived at Quench-heart Keep lies before you, its face a mask of horror. If you have the skill of Climbing, you may wish to crawl across the ceiling in the darkness away from the torch (turn to **358**). Otherwise, you step forward, ready to give battle (turn to **373**).

384

Your foot slams into his solar plexus with incredible force, cracking a rib and driving the breath from his body. He doubles up, unable to move and you lash out with a Forked Lightning strike, slamming your foot into his midriff again and then up to his throat in one swift fluid movement. He drops dead to the muddy street three seconds after your attack began. Wasting no time, you strip him of his scarlet uniform and put it on over your Ninja costume. Walking with calm assurance you enter the sleeping quarters of the monastery unchallenged and make your way to the Hall of Webs. Turn to **368**.

385

You drag your grappling hook and rope from a pocket of your costume which is now filled with slime and hurl the hook at a gnarled stump at the edge of the path. At the second attempt it holds and, looking warily for the beast tracking you to reappear, you pull yourself out of the quagmire. As you free the hook and replace it, you catch sight of the dark hulk of the beast behind you on the path, a huge warty Troll, but it doesn't advance. Suddenly the swamp erupts into the air before you and rasping fibrous tentacles slither around you. A misshapen growth like a green boulder, a Shaggoth, is attacking you. You dodge one of its tentacles and punch the heaving green mass of its body. Your fist sinks in, to little effect. Do you have any Inner Force left? If you have, turn to **343**. If you do not, turn to **327**.

386

You can hear nothing inside the room and you oil the hinges of the oak door before sliding it gently open. Yaemon, Grandmaster of Flame of the order of the Scarlet Mantis is within, meditating crosslegged on the floor. He is wearing the scarlet fighting dress of a martial arts monk, and a black cotton belt. His face is stern and impassive as he stands and bows to you. 'Welcome, Ninja. You are Avenger and I killed your spiritual father,' he says. You bow in turn and leap to the attack. Yaemon proves himself to be a peerless fighter, kicking, punching and blocking with dazzling speed and power, but your controlled hatred spurs you to great feats. Yaemon is hard-pressed until you hear footsteps on the staircase below. The red eye was a spell cast by Manse the Deathmage. He saw you through the disembodied eye and he enters the chamber behind you. You turn to aim a kick at him but he lets a green gem fall to the floor between you. He speaks an arcane word of power and the gem expands until you find yourself inside it. You cannot break out and the gem begins to contract, you shrink with it until you are the size of an ant. Manse the Deathmage smiles as he picks the gem up from the floor and you hear him remarking to Yaemon that he will have you mounted in a ring. You will live for a long time, a miniature madman on the hand of the Deathmage.

387

The mail-clad rider stiffens as you chop his neck and rolls sideways off his horse. You balance on your hands and move yourself forwards into the saddle, grabbing the reins as the horse bolts. You are an accomplished horseman and you manage to turn the frightened beast towards the hills that circle Mortavalon. The others thunder after you, and are still behind you as you enter the hills. They begin to shout a fell incantation and you feel a sluggishness overcome you. Will you spur your horse on faster (turn to **129**) or vault from the horse and run into a cave which you see in the hillside above you (turn to **275**)?

388

The poison has no effect and you manage to descend in safety to the metal grille through which you saw a man being dropped when you first arrived at Quench-heart Keep. Turn to **398**.

389
In one swift movement you place a Poison Needle on your tongue and then spit it towards the magician's face. He tries to dodge it, his Defence against your needle is 4.

If you score more than 4, turn to **338**.
If you score 4 or less, turn to **311**.

390
Which kick will you try?

The Winged Horse? Turn to **84**.
The Forked Lightning Strike? Turn to **306**.
The Leaping Tiger? Turn to **278**.
Kwon's Flail, if you know it? Turn to **240**.

You must decide now if you wish to use Inner Force.

391
The venom of the hooded cobra is deadly and you die within minutes, your body draped across that of the Deathmage. You have failed to avenge the death of your spiritual father and Yaemon will speak the word of power at the Pillars of Change that will bind your god, Kwon, in Inferno.

392
You approach the castle at a spot where the nearest

towers on either side are a hundred feet apart. You can hear the pacing of a guard on the battlements, above the croaking of bullfrogs. You ease yourself soundlessly into the chill moat as the rain thrashes the surface around you. The noise of the bullfrogs is surprisingly loud and it is noticeable when they stop their croaking suddenly. Do you have some Essence of Firenewt? If so turn to **52**, if not turn to **91**.

393

As you sneak past the guards, still warming themselves by the fire under the canvas awning, you trigger a trap and a poison needle sticks up into the sole of your foot. If you have Immunity to Poisons turn to **388**. If you do not you fall helpless to the floor, your muscles locked in a spasm. One of the guards runs you through with his sword so that he can claim that he has been vigilant enough to slay you. You have failed your mission.

394

The Cobra Man lies spread-eagled on the sand, dead. The crowd roars with approval, as you pluck the pole from the nearby dune. You grab one end and, holding it out before you, sprint to the edge of the desert and, planting the pole in the sands, sail over the wide moat, which you notice is infested with Floating Mouths, voracious fish that are all mouth and elastic belly. You land on the wall which is the lowest part of the castle as the man dressed in blue and gold floats across the moat on a small ice floe which has broken away from the edge of the ice lake. Turn to **372**.

395

The monk is also an expert in unarmed combat and tensed for an attack from his dark assailant. His Defence against your Winged Horse kick is 6, as you grunt with an explosion of Inner Force. If you hit the monk, turn to **384**. If your attack fails, turn to **403**.

396

Before you reach the deck an arrow pierces your thigh and you stumble. You pull the barbed arrow from your flesh but the muscle is badly torn. Lose 4 Endurance and subtract one from your Kick Modifier. The Ogre, enraged, raises its spiked hammer to smash you. Will you:

Try the Winged Horse kick (turn to **332**)?
Attempt the Iron Fist punch (turn to **310**)?
Slide across the deck and use the Dragon's Tail throw (turn to **345**)?

397

All is dark on the inside of the turret, but as you look up to the door at its top you see a red eye, hanging disembodied in space. It glows and the white of the eye is horribly bloodshot. As you watch it blinks and then suddenly disappears. Will you listen at the chamber door (turn to **386**) or cross the roof of the Great Keep to the turret with the Black Whirlpool flag (turn to **130**)?

398

You drop to the wide rock-hewn tunnel beneath, gambling that your mission will be completed be-

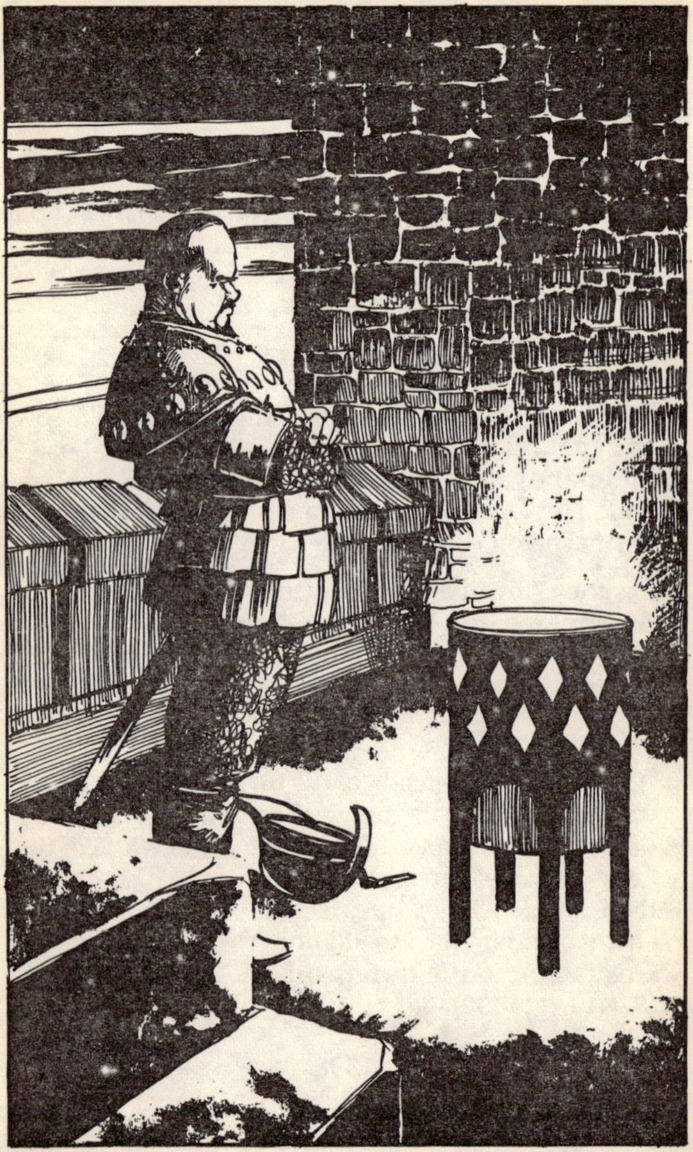

fore the guards notice that the grille is out of place. Your feet are deep in slime and squealing sewer rats brush your ankles in the darkness. You feel your way slowly and stop dead as you sense something ahead of you. It has sensed you and an ear-splitting roar echoes around the cavern which is its home. Will you continue along the tunnel towards it (turn to **383**) or, if you have the skill of Climbing and have not tried to climb in already try to leave the tunnel and scale the castle wall (turn to **392**)?

399

As you mount the staircase you see the open door to the Banqueting Hall and creep past the locked doors of the dreaming household. At last the moist wind is about you again as you peep out over the top step onto the flat roof of the Keep. The three turrets, surprisingly large now that you are so close, still boast their flags which are faintly illuminated by the glow of a charcoal brazier. With his back to this stove is the Captain of the Guard, clad in black armour. Every now and then he patrols the battlements from one turret to another before returning to warm himself at the brazier. He has taken his helmet off and is standing in the glow of the charcoals. Will you wait till he is beside the low battlements and attempt to throw him over the side (turn to **331**), use a Shuriken, aiming at his head (turn to **269**), creep up behind him and use your Garotte-wire (turn to **247**) or if you have the skill with Poison Needles will you use one (turn to **230**)?

400

Using the Iron Fist you smash Manse's head so hard that it almost flies off his shoulders. As you hear the crack as his neck breaks you feel the fangs of the cobra in your neck. The venom courses into your veins. Do you have Immunity to Poisons? If you do turn to **246**, if you do not turn to **391**.

401
Yaemon is too quick for you to have any hope with the Teeth of the Tiger, so will you try the Whirlpool throw (turn to **367**) or the Dragon's Tail throw (turn to **228**)?

You must decide now if you wish to use Inner Force.

402
You lift the grille at the moat's edge and lower yourself into the wide rock-hewn tunnel beneath, gambling that your mission will be completed before the guards notice that the grille is out of place. Your feet are deep in slime and squealing sewer rats brush your ankles in the darkness. You feel your way slowly and stop dead as you sense something ahead of you. It has sensed you, and an ear-splitting roar echoes around the cavern which is its home. Will you continue along the tunnel towards it (turn to **383**) or, if you have the skill of Climbing, leave the tunnel and try to scale the castle wall (turn to **392**)?

403
The monk is an expert in unarmed combat. He steps back and slaps your foot aside with his forearm, and then cries in panic, 'NINJA!', giving the alarm. You decide that to remain would imperil your mission and lose yourself quickly in the side streets, lying low in a burnt-out bakery for the night. You reflect that the monk recognised you were a Ninja and decide to leave Doomover, intent on making sure that Yaemon does not arrive at the Pillars of Change

before you. Using the disguise of a beggar you leave the city in the morning. Turn to **254**.

404

Your last step took you from the path, headlong into the swamp. You begin to sink inexorably, churning the mud which bubbles around you. Calmly, you cease moving, slowing your rate of descent. Do you have the skill of Climbing? If you do, turn to **385**. If you do not, turn to **362**.

405

The ox-cart clatters underneath you as you somersault above it, landing agilely on your feet. Before you can move further, two monks who bear the symbol of the Cross of Avatar, reversed, with a serpent twining around it, appear from doorways to either side of you. You recognise the insignia of Vile.

'It must be the Kwon worshipper,' says one. 'No-one but a monk could have avoided the cart.' They move in to the attack, adopting martial stances, as do you. There is a moment of silent confrontation, as you circle each other. Do you use the Tiger's Paw chop (turn to **353**), the Winged Horse kick (turn to **374**) or the Teeth of the Tiger throw (turn to **286**)?

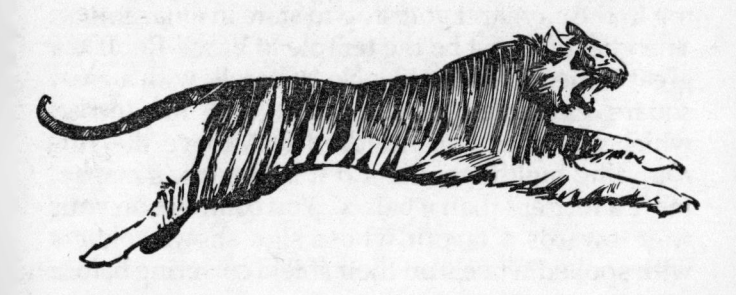

406

The lightning bolt lances past you and slams into the opposite wall, setting the planks of the hut smouldering. You leap to the attack before Olvar can unleash another. Will you try a Cobra Strike jab to his unprotected neck (turn to 377), the Winged Horse kick (turn to 302), the Dragon's Tail throw (turn to 318), or if you are skilled with Poison Needles, you may wish to use one (turn to 8)?

407

You are not fast enough and the heavy mace catches you in the face before the chop lands. Lose 8 Endurance. If you are still alive, the pain is terrible and you are knocked from the horse, landing in a heap on the ground. If you are able to slow your metabolism and Feign Death, you may turn to 376. If you cannot or will not you pick yourself up and stagger towards the river. Turn to 103.

408

You walk past the slave market where a captain of the Legion of the Sword of Doom is bidding unopposed for men to pull the oars of the ships of the Barbican League, Doomover's navy. Most of the townspeople seem to give the place a wide berth and you hurry past. You come to the largest building in the city, and you stop to stare in amazement. You guess it must be the temple to Vasch-Ro. It is a great cathedral built of blocks of basalt, with a great square embattled tower, stark and unadorned which stretches two hundred feet above the surrounding buildings. Behind it is Honoric's manse, more a fortress than a palace. You continue on your way towards a tavern whose sign shows soldiers with spoked wheels on their shield cowering before a black sword which hangs in the air. It stands inside a fork in the street and beyond it to the right you catch sight of a monastery built of dark stone with bright red shutters at its windows. It can only be a temple to Vile, the twisted brother of your God, Kwon. Might Yaemon be within? Will you:

Try the tavern as a likely source of gossip (turn to 307)?
Attempt to steal into the monastery (turn to 273)?

409

You look down at the kneeling monk and say 'I will spare you if you tell me where Yaemon, Grandmaster of the Flame, is.'

The monk has clearly lost his nerve and you believe him when he says, 'He left for the City of Druath Glennan three days ago. A large warrior went with him and I happen to know that they travel to meet another, a powerful sorcerer, I think.' You let the monk go and he walks away, head bowed. Turn to 289.

410

You bring your hand across from left to right in a vicious chop at his neck. Unfortunately he is too fast for you and he catches your wrist and delivers a deft snap-kick to your stomach. Lose 2 Endurance. If you are still alive, he places the sole of his foot onto your stomach and falls backwards, bringing you with him, straightens his leg and sends you sailing over him. Do you have Acrobatics? If you do, turn to 167. If you do not, turn to 159.

411

As his foot nears your head you drive the palm of

your right hand up onto his ankle, forcing his leg higher and he sails over your head. As you turn, he somersaults backwards to land safely on his feet and spins to face you. He runs at you to attack again. You have no time to kick, but you may try to throw him (turn to **68**), or punch him (turn to **155**).

412

The Cobra Man's strike is blindingly fast and his fangs sink into your arm, pumping a deadly venom into your veins. If you have not developed Immunity to Poisons during your training you find it suddenly difficult to breath. You fall back onto the sand and die as the roaring of blood in your ears mingles with the roar of the crowd. Your adventure is over.

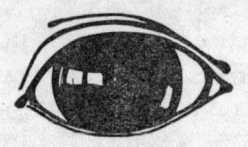

If you are immune to poison, the venom has no effect, the Cobra Man's fangs still tear your skin and you bleed, lose 2 Endurance. If you are still alive you may use the Winged Horse kick (turn to **25**), the Tiger's Paw chop (turn to **42**) or the Teeth of the Tiger throw (turn to **13**).

413

As you leap up the final few stairs he steps back and his purple lips part in a grin as he lets a small green gem tumble to the floor. It expands rapidly, threatening to engulf you. Are you an Acrobat? If you are turn to **29**. If you are not turn to **379**.

414

You stare up into the night sky until you can see in

the dark as if you were an owl, then, squeezing through the narrowest of gaps between two buildings you make your way towards the Hall of Webs which is in fact, a large hump-back bridge, thirty feet up and completely enclosed. It connects the upper floor of the sleeping quarters to the balcony of the refectory where the monks eat their meals. Standing below the window in the centre of the arch, you fit your Cat's Claws to your hands and feet and take the small grappling hook and rope from one of the inner pockets of your costume. You fling the padded hook into the open window and pull the rope taut before climbing it hand over hand, like a monkey. You are just below the window when you see a man's hands on the hook above you. Will you try to scramble the last yard up the rope before he can dislodge the hook (turn to 342) or try to dig your Claws into the flints of the bridge and climb to the side of the window (turn to 375)?

415

The guards are both blinded by the flash but cry the alarm. You see magical lights appearing around the castle like Will-O'-The-Wisps and decide to climb back down the tower, cross the moat once more and try to enter the castle through the grille that leads to an underground tunnel. Turn to **398**.

416
The hub of the wheel catches you and throws you against a wall. Lose 4 Endurance points. If you are still alive, you trudge on your way and notice some monks who bear the symbol of the Cross of Avatar, reversed with a serpent twining about it. You recognise the insignia of Vile. They ignore you and follow the cart which seems to be under control now. Turn to **289**.

417
You run on and suddenly cannot hear the splashing of the pursuing beast any more. The swamp erupts into the air before you and rasping fibrous tentacles slither round you. A mis-shapen growth like a green boulder, a Shaggoth, is attacking you. You dodge one of its tentacles and punch the heaving green mass of its body. Your fist sinks in, to little effect. Do you have any Inner Force left? If you have, turn to **343**. If you do not, turn to **327**.

418
After sketching a map of the castle from memory you conceal yourself in a hole in the ground, watching the gatehouse and wait for darkness to fall. The moon is white and full and the night is still. There is not even enough breeze to spread the banners atop the three towers. Will you choose this night to attempt to scale the derelict tower (turn to **138**), raise the grille outside the moat and drop to the tunnel below (turn to **402**) or you may decide to wait to see if the weather conditions change tomorrow night (turn to **166**)?

MAP OF QUENCH-HEART KEEP

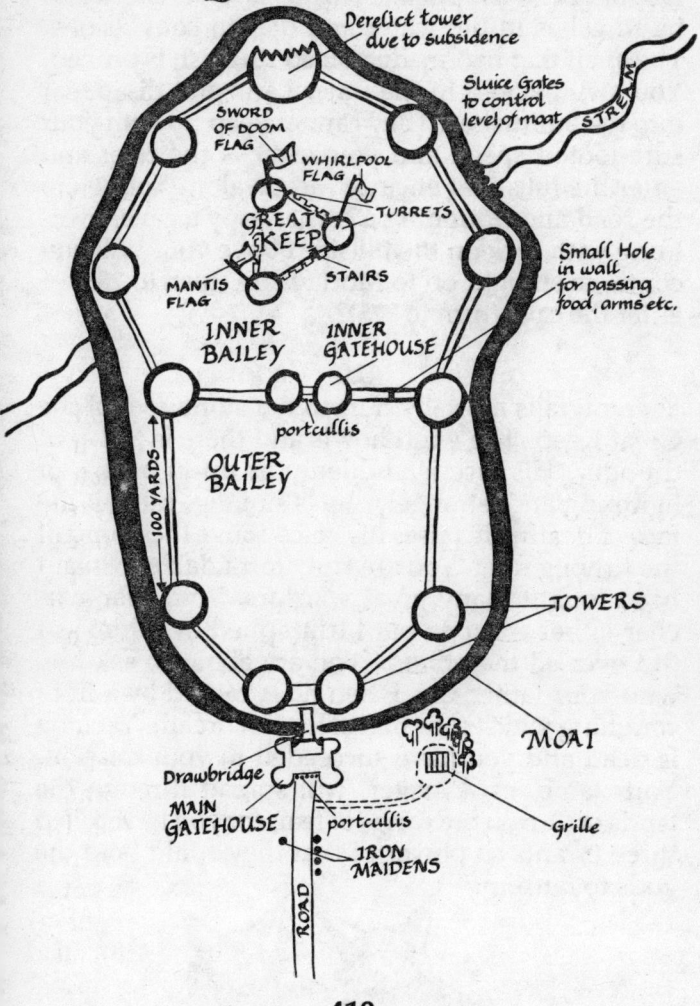

419

You thrash around in the water, pretending that you cannot swim and when they are close blow a poison needle through your breathing tube at the face of one of the priests. It slaps into his cheek and he thrashes in the water and dies in convulsions. The spell that had made you so sluggish is broken. You swim across to the other bank and disappear into the bullrushes. They cannot keep up with your sure-footed speed and you re-cross the river and enter the hills that encircle Mortavalon. You rejoin the road and, rounding a corner espy a cave, overhung with rock on the hillside above you. Will you continue straight on to Mortavalon (turn to **283**) or enter the cave (turn to **275**)?

420

Yaemon falls mortally hurt to the stone roof of the Great Keep. The wind howls and there is a clap of thunder. His face is suddenly lit up in a flare of lightning and, strangely, he is smiling, calm in the face of death. He raises his voice above the sound of the driving rain: 'You are truly formidable, Ninja. I have fought many great warriors. Your Manmarcher father was one but I triumphed over him as I did over all the others.' You are about to ask him who your father was when he is racked by a fit of coughing which robs him of his last breath. Yaemon is dead and you have succeeded in your mission. Your fame, as Avenger, will spread through the lands of Orb on the wings of fear, for you have killed three tyrants so powerful that they could hold the gods to ransom.

Yaemon's scarlet jacket, now drenched with rain and sweat, has fallen open to reveal a waxed parchment, the Scrolls of Kettsuin. You are about to open this when a wondrous feeling of peace overwhelms you and the voice of your god, Kwon, sounds all around you. 'The Grandmaster of the Dawn named you well Avenger, for now it is Yaemon and not I who will languish in the lake of boiling blood in Inferno. If you had failed the Doom Legion and the monks of the Scarlet Mantis would have swept across the Manmarch aided by the priests who revere Nemesis and all mankind would have lived in terror under the evil overlords you have slain.' Your wounds are healed as if by a miracle, and new strength floods into your body as the god gives you Inner Force. You feel dazed and awed by what is happening and the sense of Kwon's goodness fills your soul with enlightenment. 'There is little time now, Avenger, for the gods of evil move against us. You must return the Scrolls of Kettsuin to their rightful place at the Temple of the Rock on the Island of Tranquil Dreams, but your journey will be beset with dangers. I will aid you; choose a skill from the Way of the Tiger which you have not yet mastered and I will grant you its knowledge. It shall be as if you had practised it from your birthing.' The god continues, 'I will aid you, but once, at a time of great danger. If you truly have need of me, say only "Kwon, redeem me", and I shall be your salvation. I will watch over you, Avenger, for it is my hope that one day you will join me in the Garden of the Gods.'

As Kwon's presence leaves you cannot stop yourself calling out, 'Who was my real father?'

It is as if the wind itself speaks to you as the voice of Kwon fades, 'It is not yet time, Avenger.'

You shiver, noticing the coldness of the rain for the first time. Kwon has departed and you are alone once more. With a shock you hear men's cries and the sound of mail-shod feet on the staircase of the Keep . . .